DIARY OF AN UNEDUCATED MAN

TO

with my very best wishes

E Fuller

Nov 2016

DIARY OF AN
UNEDUCATED MAN

An Autobiography

E. Fullerton

ARTHUR H. STOCKWELL LTD
Torrs Park, Ilfracombe, Devon, EX34 8BA
Established 1898
www.ahstockwell.co.uk

British Library Cataloguing-in-Publication Data.
A catalogue record for this book is available
from the British Library.

ISBN 978-0-7223-4318-0
Printed in Great Britain by
Arthur H. Stockwell Ltd
Torrs Park   Ilfracombe
Devon EX34 8BA

CHAPTER 1

It was a tiny room by modern standards and was overflowing with people. This sombre room and its occupants seem to have been completely forgotten during the whole of my childhood. Only as I reached middle age did the memory of it return.

The meaning and significance of this event were to become quite clear to me – the darkness of the room and the manner in which those present were dressed. The atmosphere was quiet, manifesting a general feeling of distress, but I cannot remember who was there – not even my mother, my brother and sister or any other members of the family who I am sure would have been present.

That is the only recollection I have regarding the existence of my father, although with the passing of time I have been able to recall more details of that particular day. I was three years old at the time. I recollect the upright piano with the legs bound round with cloth to preserve them from damage, this being in the only available room in the house. It is interesting that in recent years this custom of covering the legs of ones most prized possessions has been mistakenly attributed to the prudery of the Victorian era.

I did not remember the long box along one side of the room, but I do now. I also remember being lifted up to look inside the box, but I cannot to this day remember what my father looked like at his passing – a good thing perhaps!

Recalling all this, I can now understand what a terrible time

Mother and the three of us at the time of Father's passing.

this must have been for my mother, a young woman in her late twenties only, with three young children, the eldest only six years old. It is strange how the healing effect of passing time seems to have gone into reverse. Whenever I think of this occasion, I now feel some of the sadness which at the time I was too young to realise.

Throughout the following years, Mother's decision to remain single had a lasting effect on our lives. At this time we were living in Hull, somewhere off the Boulevard. Grandfather, Mother's father, was living in Grimsby, where he had gone some years earlier to work. It is not surprising therefore that after Father's death we joined Grandfather in that town.

Apart from Father's funeral, my earliest recollection is of my first day at school at the age of five. I remember looking out through the school window, and I can still visualise the large snowflakes falling – 'Santa Claus shaking his feather bed'.

Although my days at school were somewhat uneventful, I did shine at some subjects – at drawing, painting and other crafts I was always top of the class, so much so that whenever there was a competition I was not allowed to participate as the predictable conclusion was considered unfair to the rest of the class. The fact that it was unfair to me never entered the mind of the teacher, who was otherwise very fair. This incident in itself seems of little importance. It did, however, have a lasting effect on me. Long into my teens I retained a silly notion that it

The only photograph of Father.

was better to appear less able than I was. It was a little costly at times and I eventually overcame it, though never entirely.

Mother's widow's pension was hopelessly inadequate. In consequence, Mother obtained a part-time job, cleaning the house of a professional lady who lived about a mile from our home. I still find it hard to comprehend how she managed this at the same time as looking after three children and keeping house for three more adults.

When Mother along with her small brood returned to live with her father again, it was the signal to his second wife, Ada, to relinquish all household chores. To all intents and purposes Mother began a life of slavery. The house itself, inside and out, was every inch Victorian. Brass doorknobs, and an abundance of brass fireside ornaments were all to be cleaned each week; the front and rear doorsteps were to be washed and scoured with 'step-stone' (step-stone, a piece of sandstone used to clean steps, left a deposit on the step to enhance its appearance); and windows were to be washed inside and out – no window cleaners in those days.

There were no washing machines either. Instead a dolly (an implement resembling a three-legged stool with a long handle fitted to the centre) was used to agitate the washing by hand – a very arduous task. Then the clothes were put through the wringer, or mangle, which was wound by hand to remove most of the water. As we children grew older we had to take it in turns to hand-wind the wringer to take a little of the workload. I recall at one time when our cousins were staying with us for a few days' holiday one of them lost the end of a finger in the gears of the wringer. With the absence of telephones it was a quick dash on foot to the local hospital, a mile or so away – quite a traumatic event.

Grandfather was sixty-six when we joined him and Ada. He was a good man, both honest and hardworking. I suppose he could not help being, like the house he was in and the era in which he had lived all his life, Victorian. We were therefore subjected to the discipline of a time two generations back from our own. It was not the easiest of times for us.

John Roland Dickson, Grandfather, 1926.

According to Grandfather, children were to be seen and not heard. Our life was therefore not as happy as that of other children of our time. To this day I still hear on occasions someone say to a child, "Schooldays are the best days of your life. Make the most of them." As a child I could never understand this advice, which was given to me on many occasions. If these were the best days of my life, I could not help thinking that I was in for a very rough ride indeed!

Even at the age of sixty-six the old man, bless his heart, walked the four miles to work and back every day and continued to do so until the age of seventy-three – the age at which he eventually retired. As an engineering craftsman, he stood over a centre lathe all day, and then the walk must have made him very tired at the end of the day. No doubt this is what made him a little intolerant of us children. That, I suppose, is why we were condemned to bed every evening at the early hour of seven o'clock, winter and summer.

How well I remember those nights my brother and I spent in that cold bedroom! We lay awake for hours on end every night talking in whispers so as not to be heard. There was no radio or other entertainment to break the silence of those days – or should I say 'nights'. Any sound of movement or other noise brought some response from below – usually a threat of some kind or another, which to us at the time seemed real enough. In the summertime we could hear the other children playing outside in the street under our window. On odd occasions we would sneak a look behind the curtains to see what was going on. We often received a scolding when one of the children outside (who knew of our internment) took it upon himself to knock on our door and report our misdemeanour.

Getting washed and ready for bed for seven o'clock meant our day effectively ended at six thirty and left us very little time to play. Often after arriving home from school we were sent out again to the shops – a further encroachment on our meagre playing time, made worse by the fact that we sometimes had to go not to the nearest shops, but to one farther away as it was a little cheaper. Our journeys to and from school four times a day were timed almost to the minute, as indeed were our journeys to the shops. All in all, we often found we had no time to play at all.

When six o'clock arrived, the adults sat down to the evening meal. We were expected to sit quietly on a wooden bench until they had finished. This was mental torture, and I well remember the day when Mother could not tolerate the situation any longer and we were allowed to play in the small garden or the scullery, depending on the weather, until it was our turn at the table. Not once, as I remember, did we ever sit at the table with the adults.

The Victorian house had only three bedrooms, but, as far as I remember, they were large rooms with high ceilings. The ground floor consisted of the 'front room' (the holy of holies), the living room and a large scullery. The scullery had a walk-in pantry along with a 'wash house', also of ample proportions.

The wash house had in it a huge cast-iron basin known as a 'copper'. I assume it got its name from the fact that in the more well-to-do houses it would have been made out of that material – copper! This cast-iron vessel was surrounded by a very large brick structure in which was fashioned a fire grate. You've guessed it – it was for boiling the clothes on washday, and was fitted with a large, heavy wooden lid. Almost everything in those days seemed to be big and heavy, and mostly made of cast iron or wood. This huge 'copper' took up almost half the wash house; the remainder was used to store the coal, which was delivered half a ton at a time. Not surprisingly it had come to be known as 'the coalhouse'. Now, this 'wash house-cum-coalhouse' had a window which hadn't had a pane of glass in it for donkey's years. It was not a small window, as one might assume because of the absence of glass, but large enough to admit any intruder who may have been inclined to enter. This, I think, speaks well for the times in which we lived! The only obstacle was the chicken wire nailed over the hole. Ventilation obviously was more important than security. The reader will see the significance of this window as my story unfolds.

Also on the ground floor of our Victorian home we had a flushing lavatory – or water closet, as we called it. It was outside in the yard, which was part of the small garden. This garden, for us children, became literally our prison for many years.

Roomy though the house was, it did not have any electricity. I think we were the only ones in that area whose home was illuminated by gaslight. I use the word 'illuminated' lightly (forgive the unintended pun). Although most rooms were fitted with gaslight fittings, only one room in the house was ever lit on a daily basis. That was the living room; all the other rooms remained in darkness – except the scullery, which was lit by a single candle, but only during the early evening when the evening meal was being prepared and for the subsequent washing-up. After that it was 'lights out' to save the candle.

One evening, when all the activity was at an end, I was chosen to retrieve the candle from the scullery. I vividly remember that night as though it were yesterday. I was very young at the time and I was scared stiff of the dark – terrified, in fact! That night I received the fright of my life.

At work Grandfather always wore full-length overalls, and of course they became very dirty. But Mother knew exactly how to deal with them. She laid them on the ground in the backyard, scrubbed them with a strong yard brush (using Parazone, a well-known bleach of the day) and boiled them in the giant copper. They came out almost white.

This night, when little Teddy (that was me) was detailed to rescue the candle, Mother had hung the overalls on the edge of the coalhouse door. She was relying, I suppose, on the breeze from the permanently open window to dry them. Well, little Teddy wasn't expecting this; he didn't know about the overalls hung up to dry. Notwithstanding the fact that he was scared about walking along the dark corridor, he passed the walk-in pantry and went down the step into the cold and gloomy scullery, with only the flickering light of the candle to guide him. It was then that he spotted the whitish overalls, with one leg at one side of the door and the other, fully inflated by the breeze, at the other side of the door. Breeze indeed – the wind was literally howling like a banshee, adding a little more to the spooky situation! When the inflated leg appeared to take a step forward, it was time for little Teddy to run. Without taking his eyes off the apparition, he made a grab for the candle, missed it and burnt his finger. The candle finished up on the floor. He was now in a blind panic. Before he could even turn to run, however, there was an almighty ear-shattering noise behind him as the roller blind which covered the scullery window (one with glass in it) decided to add a little more atmosphere to the scene: it flew up the window.

I reached the living room in record time, shaking as I had never shaken before and feeling quite limp. Mother was also quite shaken when she saw the state I was in, but the pampering which followed was soon, to my embarrassment, replaced by laughter.

CHAPTER 2

My aptitude for drawing, etc., as mentioned, was due to the fact that we had virtually no toys to speak of. Paper, pencils and crayons were the things which kept us occupied and, more importantly, quiet. After each Christmas we were given the Christmas cards, which provided us with paper to draw on as well as pictures to copy.

In spite of our lack of funds, we were always kept clean and well dressed – perhaps too clean, as I remember – and few people realised that we did not have a father. Indeed, keeping up appearances was very important to Mother, and no one worked harder on that than she. That did not, however, make our lives any easier – quite the reverse, in fact. On arriving home from school each evening we were subjected to a rigorous scrutiny. A little dirt, not to mention a tear in our clothes, caused a scene which is easy to remember. Our shoes in particular came in for a most thorough examination, and woe betide us if we had a scuff mark! This brought the inevitable accusation that we had kicked something, and deliberately too! Imagine that – a schoolboy playing football, perhaps! Little wonder that I never came to understand or like football, although, like all kids, I shared the urge to kick a stone or something on the way home.

For most kids, walking was the only way to travel, and the streets were simply there to play in. These days it is quite impossible to visualise the streets as they were before motor cars became so numerous. Every day one could see two boys,

12

one at each side of the street, kicking a ball (or a substitute for a ball) from one side to the other with little or no interference from traffic. Cricket as well as football was played in the street, as was skipping, the rope often spanning the full width of the street. These activities were interrupted only by the occasional horse-drawn cart.

These carts were a source of delight as boys often climbed on to the backs of the slow-moving vehicles and stole a ride. Most drivers tolerated this lark, provided that the boys sat quietly at the back. A few choice words from the drivers who didn't approve quickly caused the culprits to scamper off. What villains the boys were in those days!

In spite of everything it was, I think, a good time to be young! Most people were hard up. Even those in work found it hard to make ends meet. Nevertheless most seemed to be happy. Crime was not unheard of, but most people seemed far more honest than their counterparts today. Few people ever locked their doors, day or night.

There were not so many policemen in those days. The few we had mainly *walked* the beat. A clip across the ear from the local bobby was enough to keep most youngsters on the right side of the law. What I think was more important is that mothers seldom went out to work; they were always there when their children came home from school. Children therefore spent less time getting into mischief on the streets. On the whole, discipline, both in school and at home, was neither harsh nor unjust. It was simply consistent. Ours – dare I say it? – was a little on the heavy side!

Thieving, violence, coarse language and envy were not commonplace, as they are today. Also the penalty for crime was a real deterrent. Hard labour and a hard time in jail kept the jails small and less crowded, and the birch too made potential thugs think twice about offending.

The police at that time were held in great respect, as indeed were teachers. The latter, who were always dressed smartly, actually taught children both respect towards others and self-respect. It is not so today. Regrettably many teachers dress like tramps – the scruffier the better, it seems! This, coupled with the foolish notion of encouraging their charges to address them by their Christian names and drop the 'sir' or 'Miss', is in itself a contributory factor for the slovenly, unattractive morals and decay so predominant today.

Although I look back with nostalgia to the football and other street games, I remember them as an observer rather than as one of those who joined in. It is one of the few things for which I feel no gratitude towards Mother and Grandfather. The freedom of playing in the street was never allowed us. Involvement in some game or other on the way home, or even a leisurely walk home from school, was, as I mentioned earlier, not for us. Home at the allotted time, we endured the inevitable inspection and were then confined to the backyard for the short period remaining before bedtime. These were supposed to be the best years of my life! The mistaken decision to protect us from the influence and danger of mixing with youngsters of our generation was to cause us problems in later life, which far outweighed the imagined dangers perceived at the time. I have no wish to inflict on the reader a long and detailed account of the problems this misguided policy caused me and my brother through almost all our remaining years; suffice it to say, they have not been easy to overcome.

Living, as one might say, on the breadline, our diet was anything but mouth-watering! Breakfast never varied from one year to the next. It consisted of porridge made with water and very little sugar and never with fresh milk! Fresh milk was only seen in the house if one of us was ill. Sweet tinned condensed milk was the additive used to make tea drinkable; and as this was what the adults drank. We thought for years that everyone else did likewise, as in truth many people did.

Being ill did have its compensations! Porridge was not the only thing which suddenly became a real treat. Rice pudding, hitherto tasting similar to the gruel porridge, also became scrumptious! Butter – 'best butter', as it was known to us – never saw the light of day in our house. It was always margarine for us. We did, however, have the option of jam, but it was one or the other, margarine or jam, never the two together – something we would have enjoyed! Anyone who has tasted jam alone on bread will know just how unpalatable it can be! One thing I promised myself when I was very young was that when I grew up I would never eat margarine again.

I regularly paid an unofficial visit to the pantry, as did my brother. In the absence of sweets, we used to help ourselves to sugar and a fair amount of condensed milk. This often provoked Ada (Grandfather's second wife) to a loud and lengthy sermon on the fact that the sugar and the tinned milk did not seem to be lasting as long as they used to! This usually resulted in the sugar and the milk lasting longer, but the improvement would be only temporary. The sequence of stealing and sermon became a regular feature of our existence.

On some of these visits to the pantry I found six scones standing there on a plate with lashings of cream bulging out on all sides. It was a temptation beyond my resistance. Luxuries, like pastries, were only seen in the house at weekends and only for the adults. A quick journey around each scone with my finger allowed me to sample the delights of the forbidden fruit! It was of course necessary to restore the scones to their former appearance, but this was easy enough to do. Slight pressure applied to the top of the bun caused the cream to bulge out all around once more! It never occurred to me that the thickness of the cream was somewhat diminished. I was convinced that things looked just the same. It was inevitable that the shrinking buns would be noticed, but due to the ecstasy of the moment that thought never entered my head. What is more, it never entered my head that my brother might be doing the same thing!

Eventually the scones became so depleted of cream that Ada threw a fit. Atom bombs and volcanoes came a poor second to Ada when she really had something to have a go at.

"Just look at these scones!" she exploded. "There used to be a lot more cream when we first started buying them. I'm going to see that Mr Melton myself and I'll tell him."

Mr Melton owned the grocery shop just three doors away at the street corner. He was not unaccustomed to the old woman's somewhat direct approach when she considered she was getting a poor deal!

I could never understand why we were never tackled regarding this misdemeanour. I guess I probably would not be here today if we had been rumbled.

Ada had everything worked out to the last farthing (one eighth of a penny, for the scholars of today). Every weekend one of us children would be instructed to fetch the weekly grocery bill from Melton's. This was then given the utmost scrutiny, worthy of any income-tax inspector. If there was an error, or if Ada thought there was an error, it was one of us who had the task of negotiating between the two. Back and forth we would go until Ada won.

As far as I can remember Mr Melton only ever won one round of these tournaments. It was, in fact, I who brought about this historic event.

It was midsummer and our cousins had come to stay with us for a few days. This was something we children looked forward to very much. Not only did we have someone to play with, but we were allowed to play outside in the street – the reason being that our cousins, like all other children except us, were accustomed to this freedom.

A little further down the street from our house, on the other side of the street, was a vacant plot of land known locally as Pig's Field. It was very much overgrown and an ideal place for adventure. It was not very long before we decided that a bonfire would be the order of the day and we all set about collecting the necessary sticks, etc. It was only after a good-sized heap was established that we realised that we needed some means of ignition. The few men who passed by refused our polite request for the necessary match. Now, our cousins knew about Ada's weekly account at the local shop, and they also knew that I had access to it, so against my better judgement I allowed myself to be coerced into getting the matches on Ada's account. Not showing a morsel of fear, like Albert in that famous monologue 'The Lion and Albert', I presented myself at the shop and Mr Melton produced the goods without any to-do.

That day turned out to be very happy. In fact it eventually turned out to be unforgettable! The leftover matches were hidden for future use and the incident of the bonfire and the matches was soon forgotten. Well, that is until the weekend! Our playmates by this time had returned home and yes, sir, the day of reckoning was nigh. My sins were about to catch up with me!

At the appointed time Ada was presented with the weekly bill, and there are no prizes for guessing who it was who had the honour of presenting it to her. For some reason I was not feeling very courageous as I handed over the evidence. I had the distinct notion that something very dreadful was about to happen to me.

"What's this? Take this back to Mr Melton and tell him that I did not have a box of matches this week."

I wasn't too happy about facing Mr Melton, but there was no way that I could withdraw from the impending conflict. On my return to the shop Mr Melton assured me that Grandma (not the name we had for the old witch) had had the aforesaid item and – would you believe it? – he even remembered who had asked for them! The walk back home from the shop, just three doors away, took a little longer than usual. Silly when you think about it – prolonging the agony like that!

Eventually I found myself confronting Her Grace – or, more correctly, she was confronting me.

Pulling myself up to my full height, I looked her straight in her ample abdomen, but before I could raise a feeble squeak, she demanded, "What did he say, then? Has he crossed it off?"

"N-no" came my somewhat quiet reply.

I don't think she heard me. In any case, it was obvious that here was the making of an encounter that was very much to her liking.

"Come on," she said. "You're coming with me."

She was out of her chair in a flash. I had never seen her move so fast before. Because of her size (just over five feet in both directions) she usually needed a few minutes to vacate a chair, so I knew right away that she wasn't happy. I wasn't too happy myself – it was becoming more and more obvious that I was about to admit to my misdemeanour. That was terrifying enough, but the very thought of interfering with Ada when she was in full sail, and denying her the satisfaction of putting Mr Melton in his place, was something to contemplate, I can tell you!

We were outside the shop before she realised that I was trying to say something. Talk about the lull before the storm! My almost inaudible utterances were first met with stony silence, as the magnitude of my sin and the frustration of having to retreat from what she was sure was certain victory (the very highlight of her day) took hold of her.

"This is what comes of letting you out of our sight! You'll stop in the garden in future." She said this in a tone which suggested that it was a special punishment and not the normal state of affairs.

The one advantage of having no privileges is that we had nothing to lose. Nevertheless for some time I kept behind the wallpaper (out of sight) – a favourite saying used by my wife's father many years later.

A box of matches at that time cost the equivalent of a quarter of a new penny, and that just happened to be the amount we received as pocket money each week. Why my pocket money was not stopped on the week of our bonfire I do not know, but I was grateful about that. Our weekly pocket money bought us six or seven boiled sweets. It was always boiled sweets as we were under orders: "Don't spend it on anything wasteful" – Ada's free advice when dispensing the allowance. She insisted on our buying something *she* liked, as we had to hand them round before we ourselves could partake of the luxuries! On our way home from the shop it was our cunning custom to sort out the sweets by size, making sure that the smallest were on the top. Sometimes when doing this we dropped one on the ground, and that one was always on the top when we presented them to the dear old lady. If she picked the one with the added flavour we scored a victory! When offering the sweets around I cannot remember either Mother or Grandfather taking one, but Ada, as I recall, seldom refused.

Whilst on the subject of high finance I clearly remember finding twopence. It does not seem a lot, but that was four weeks' pocket money! After a windfall of this magnitude, both my brother and sister were sworn to secrecy. The money was spent surreptitiously on the way to school and lasted several days. In that way the proceeds were eaten without fear of discovery. Secrecy was paramount as otherwise the loot would have gone into the communal money box, as did any coppers given to us by friends or relatives. Indeed every penny from whatever source went into the box towards our clothes. We did not appreciate it at the time, but Mother must have been pretty desperate for money during those difficult days.

In spite of our situation Mother never asked for, and never received, any kind of charity. She was far too proud for that. I can't help thinking, though, that if we had been consulted about it we might just have said, "Yes, please."

Once in a while Mother would take the three of us to visit some relative or other. We all looked forward to these visits, although we always felt very shy and found it a little hard to communicate. This was owing to the permanent isolation in which we were kept. Nevertheless we enjoyed playing with the children of the house and their many toys.

Mealtimes were a bit of a trial because of our timidity, but we tucked in to the bread and 'best butter' – so much so that on many occasions our host was heard to remark, "I have never seen children who enjoyed bread and butter so much."

We never attempted to explain why this was so – dignity, you see!

Mrs Diamond, a nice lady who lived next door, had a part-time job in a local bakery, and because she was aware of our situation she used to bring us surplus trimmings from some kind of cake. This was at one time a weekly occurrence. However, our loving step-grandmother decided that the donation was for her benefit and the goodies were eaten by her and Grandfather. We had but a tiny taste. It was not surprising therefore that through Mrs Diamond's daughter, who was of our generation, we dropped the hint to our benefactor and the treats promptly stopped.

CHAPTER 3

Life for us kids, literally prisoners in the garden day after day, was, to say the least, a little monotonous. A change of any sort from the routine was always welcome. The one really fabulous event was the annual trip back to Hull. This came about because Grandfather took a holiday with his friends once a year, just for one week. One week was the norm for working people back then. It was doubly exiting for us as we stayed with our cousins. Their house was very tiny and the three of us slept in the same bed as our three cousins – three at the top and three at the bottom. It was great fun and we loved it. What is more, with the house being so tiny we had to play outdoors – another real treat!

As I have said, although we looked forward very much to our brief change of lifestyle, our first introduction to Aunt Maggie's home (she was a lovely person) was without doubt a real culture shock. Back home, in spite of our personal circumstances we lived in a much larger house. We took the small garden and the flushing lavatory (though it was outside in the yard) to be normal.

Auntie's house was very different. There were just two rooms upstairs and two down, with the tiniest yard we had ever seen. I estimate that it was no more than ten feet by ten feet.

By far the biggest shock was the lavatory. Although the wooden seat was scrubbed almost white, and the small cupboard-like room was also very clean, it was what was known as an 'earth closet'. We had never heard of such a thing and we hated having to use it. As far as I can remember, this closet consisted of a square metal tank with a handle at each end. This was placed against the back wall. Over the top of the tank, fixed at each end into the side walls, was the seat. This was a heavy plank of wood, very thick and with a hole in the centre. Each week the tank was taken from under the plank, carried out of the yard into the street, and emptied into a huge tank which was fitted with two large wheels and a large horse. The whole affair seemed absolutely disgusting, and we felt sorry for the men who earned a living this way.

It was even more surprising to us when we discovered that just a street or two away things were even worse. Some of the houses, we were told, were built back to back and were known as 'back-to-backs'. This meant that the houses had no rear entrance, and in consequence the disgusting cargo had to be carried through the houses to be disposed of. The very thought of that made us shudder, and we realised that in spite of our difficulties we were almost posh by comparison. To add to our disbelief, it was also revealed that other houses nearby actually shared outside closets with their neighbours. Looking back to this time, round about 1927, I still marvel that this situation existed such a short time ago.

The journey from Grimsby to Hull, and the return journey, rivalled the holiday itself for excitement and enjoyment. The journey by steam train was very different from a similar train journey of today. Almost every town and village had a station, and the trains were slower, which was nice. During these leisurely trips our eyes never left the ever changing scenery as it passed by the windows. We soon got to know every station along the way, passing as we did every year. The trains in those days stopped at every station without exception, often for some considerable time. Goods of all descriptions as well as some livestock made up the normal load, and the bustle on the platform was very interesting to watch. This was before the building of the Humber Bridge, though the idea was often talked about. Grandfather said it would never happen.

The only way across the river was by the ferry. This was a

particular delight for us. Although the actual journey time was about twenty minutes (provided the boat didn't become stranded on a sandbank, as it often did), the loading and unloading took longer. This was owing once more to the goods and livestock also making the journey. Once under way, there was still a lot to see. The city, for instance, looked very different from the middle of the river. As the boat splashed its way over the water we could watch the steam engine huffing and puffing as it turned the massive paddles, and we could also watch the man who looked after the engine, who oiled it and polished it all the way to his pension.

It is hard to believe that the enormous amount of change which has taken place since my schooldays has happened in less than a lifetime. Nothing illustrates this better than the scene we observed on our arrival by the ferry at the Hull pier. The pier itself was a good place to visit, and the good people of Hull were not in ignorance of this. Most days the upper and lower decks of this Victorian extravagance was awash with people of all ages. It was the end of the road and a turnaround point for the trams, which arrived and departed at very frequent intervals. A very lasting impression was made by the hansom cabs which were parked all around the area of the pier. Horses and drivers were all spruced up, giving a comfortable and leisurely atmosphere to the whole scene. Taxis were in evidence, but these were few and far between as the motor car was still an alien upstart. It was unthinkable that it could ever replace the more gentle and aristocratic cab, which had been plying its trade for centuries!

Everything and everybody moved at an unhurried, almost sleepy, pace. Remnants of the recent Victorian age were very much in evidence. The women wore dresses, mostly black in colour, which reached down to their feet. For the men, bowler hats were still the height of fashion alongside the flat caps, and many sported a gold watch and chain stretched across the front of their waistcoats. The whole area of the pier was flanked on all sides by trees, so that, along with cabs, the snoozing horses and their unflappable drivers, it was serenity all the way.

For some years it was a hansom cab which took us between the pier and Aunt Maggie's and I have cause to remember the first time we ventured into modern times by way of the taxi. I sat next to the door to make sure I missed nothing. We were just passing the statue of King William (King Billy, as he was known locally), and Grandfather had informed us that the King always climbed down from his horse and went into the local pub for a drink when the clock struck twelve. While contemplating this I was hanging on to the handle on the door, which I thought was there for that purpose. I realised that was not the case long before Mother, in a blind panic, picked me up from the middle of the road. Had the traffic conditions of the time been anything like the conditions prevailing today it would not have been the relatively minor incident it turned out to be.

This little episode happened in Queen Street, one of the oldest streets of the old town. This street in those days was a hive of activity. The whole of the street was lined with handcarts which sported canvas covers or awnings. Every kind of fruit and vegetable, along with pots, pans and a wide variety of other goods, were piled up on these carts; it truly was a bazaar of sorts, with people falling over one another because of their numbers.

At night it was more like fairyland, every cart having its own method of illumination. Oil lamps and gas lamps were in profusion, and we thought it was great.

Queen Street then was composed of nothing but shops and the odd public house. The shops were for the most part converted dwelling houses, all of which had seen better times. I was not aware of that at the time. It was in later years that I became aware of the splendid architecture of the grand houses. Regretfully, most of them fell into decay because of planning blight caused by the misguided town council of later times. It is only in recent years that a more enlightened policy has prevailed and the street has become at least respectable again. Sadly, however, the character of the street, now lined with modern buildings, has gone for ever.

Our visits to Hull were the most interesting and happiest of times. This otherwise fine city had perhaps more than its fair share of slums – a problem which did not begin to be rectified until many years later. Nevertheless we considered it full to overflowing with things and places of interest. I recall that there were at least six museums in addition to the art gallery, all of which were free from admission fees. By far the grandest of these was the one in Albion Street. Regrettably this was completely destroyed by Adolf Hitler during the Second World War, and the site, even at this late date, is still nothing more than a car park. From the best-known museum to the smallest and least known: this was situated in the Paragon Station and the entrance was through a small door in the main hall, seldom noticed by the many who passed its portals even on a daily basis. The small door led directly to the narrowest of staircases, similar to those of a small dwelling house, and the exhibits were, as might be guessed, all appertaining to railways. Paragon Station at that time had another item of interest: namely, a life-sized replica of Stevenson's Rocket, one of the first steam trains. This replica was for many years resident in the centre of the main hall. I often wonder what became of it. No doubt it was the changing times which prompted its eventual removal.

Hull fascinated us children. I realise that to a great extent this was due to the extra freedom we enjoyed. However, the parks here were larger and contained much that kept us occupied, sometimes past the allotted time for our return home. The swings and roundabouts – things which we had not seen before – were an endless source of delight. Indeed, the pleasures seemed endless. After the free swings, etc., there were the large lakes with numerous ducks and other birds – even swans, would you believe? Also, many of the parks had aviaries, aquariums, and miniature zoos. All this we packed into seven glorious days.

The memories of those early visits to Hull come flooding back, but there is one little episode in particular which will always remain in my memory. It clearly emphasises that it truly was a time of relative innocence. Imagine if you can what obscenities one might overhear if what I am about to repeat was encountered on the streets of today. Two little boys were having an altercation with a third, and one of the boys is called Herbert. Herbert's little friend, in an attempt to show his utter contempt for the situation and to be as obscene as he can, advises his little friend with the immortal words, "Pee on 'im, 'Erb." This true story illustrates, I think, the vast difference between the street talk of those days and that which is so commonplace today. So sad!

A few years later at the age of twelve we returned to Hull to live. This was because Grandfather, who had returned to Hull to live following his retirement, had died, and Mother made a bad decision to return to look after Ada. Mother really was one for punishment! I say Mother's choice was a bad one, not because we were reluctant to become residents of what hitherto was our holiday venue, but because we were so much better off where we were. When Grandfather and Ada first decided to return to the city, Mother had made the monumental decision to remain in Grimsby. We just could not believe our luck when this happened. At a stroke we were free, just like other children, and when Grandfather died we were just becoming accustomed to this freedom and making friends.

The following years were full of change. The house in which we now found ourselves, though clean, was in a so-called slum area and was due for demolition. The good thing was that we were only there for some eighteen months, after which we were allocated a brand-new house in the east of the city. We felt that we had really landed in paradise – hot and cold running water, a bathroom, electricity and an inside toilet. The fact that we had to change schools once again did not, after all, seem so bad.

At first our move from Grimsby to Hull was not at all to our liking. In the short time that we had been running free, as it were, we had made many friends. Leaving one little girl in particular caused me much pain. It seems she was my 'first awakening' and I remember her to this day.

I missed also singing in the church choir. It was a men's choir, my brother and I being the only boy members. At Christmas time the choir travelled the streets of Grimsby, singing carols. They were such happy times, and we were reluctant to make the break.

Our new house with its modern facilities, however, helped us to settle down and enjoy our new beginning. The short spell in the old house as well as the short stay at the new school, which we did not like at all, were soon forgotten.

This change for the better in our lifestyle was enhanced somewhat by the fact that our new school was similar to the small church school from which we had been so painfully extracted. In fact, the new school and adjacent church were almost a replica of the ones in Grimsby. Consequently we soon settled down and once more became the only boy members of the adult choir.

I was blessed with what those around me claimed was a good singing voice, and it was because of this affliction that we were cajoled into singing in the said choirs. I should have been pleased with the attention this gave me, but I wasn't. At that time I was timidity itself – something which stayed with me to some extent until the time of my war service.

War, as we all know, changes many things and many people, and I was no exception. It rid me of my timidity, and for that I am eternally grateful. I returned to Civvy Street with a new-found confidence, the extent of which I did not fully realise until many years later as I became successful in my business ventures.

When I eventually started in business I was absolutely penniless. I literally had no savings at all! How's that for confidence – or was it arrogance? I prefer to think not, for some of the shyness born of my upbringing still remains with me. Nevertheless, as the reader will learn, I did in fact become quite successful, acquiring as I did assets of over £3 million. Perhaps if I had been a little more arrogant, and perhaps a little less generous, I would not have lost most of it sometime after my retirement.

It was at the age of fourteen years that my schooldays came to an end, and I ventured out into the big wide world. To me that is just what it appeared to be. Standing all of four feet ten inches (one and a half metres), or perhaps a little less, and feeling as timid as it is possible to feel, I set out to find myself a job. Although I started off with some enthusiasm, I very soon became more than a little despondent – so much so that I spent much of my time wandering aimlessly around the town.

'Aimlessly' is not the right word, for I was utterly fascinated. There was indeed much going on and plenty to hold my interest. It was a time of great change – the city centre was being changed beyond belief. The very large Queen's Dock was being filled in and was about to become the Queen's Gardens, as they are known today. R. G. Tarran, a local bigwig and benefactor in building, was busy dismantling the monument to William Wilberforce and moving it to its new site at the far end of the said gardens. He did this free, gratis and for nowt – well, he said it was for nowt. Monument Bridge, which divided Whitefriargate and all things east from the rest of the city centre, was the original site of the statue. The bridge too was being removed along with the dock, and Hull was about to lose a most picturesque feature. Queen's Gardens today seems a nice enough place, but I cannot help feeling that a rare and wonderful opportunity for some imaginative planning was missed and lost for ever. Now, more than eighty years later, nothing has changed. Poor planning is still the norm, as is borne out by the new logo (The Cog) which some bright spark is trying to sell us.

The despondency to which I referred earlier was brought about by my stature, or should I say lack of it? "Sorry – you are too small", or words to that effect, greeted me whenever I plucked up the courage to make an application for work. However, I eventually obtained employment, starting work as a pageboy. It can never be said that I started off from anything but a small beginning.

The Regal Cinema in Ferensway was the newest and the largest of its kind. Well, it had to be. You see, it was built by that previously mentioned bigwig, R. G. Tarran. It turned out that Mr Tarran was a director of County Cinemas, the consortium (big word for me, that!) which owned not only the Regal, but also the Regis, Hessle High Road; the Royalty, Southcoates Lane; the Rex, North Hull Estate; and the Astoria, Holderness High Road, along with others in various cities in Yorkshire.

The Regal in its heyday was really something. This was, of course, before the advent of television, which put the lid on Pandora's box, so to speak. With its huge vestibule (posh word for entrance) and a foyer big enough to play football in, along with broad staircases, it was most impressive! I thought so anyway. There was a café on the first floor, opposite the entrance to the circle. On the next floor up was the Regal Room and the Regal Room Foyer, to mention just two of the function rooms, not all of which were ever used. There was an enormous stage and it was easy to get lost in the labyrinth of dressing rooms and other rooms containing technical paraphernalia.

My beginnings as a pageboy, 1935.

My day started at nine in the morning and went on until the same time at night. The mornings were spent cleaning oceans of brasswork and performing other equally boring cleaning jobs. From lunchtime onwards, dressed in a white dicky and black bow tie, I, along with another two 'slaves', opened doors, ran errands, tore up tickets by the bucketful and talked to customers. All in all it was a most skilful and exacting occupation, don't you think? This job as a pageboy, though a real dogsbody of a job, appealed to me at the time, and I was very happy. This was at a time when cinemas were not allowed to open on Sundays, except, that is, for charity concerts, of which there were many throughout the year. At such times many big names in show business, including film stars from as far away as Hollywood, often visited us. I enjoyed these particular evenings – working back stage unpaid, but meeting all the stars.

I was enjoying things so much that I lost sight of the fact that it was a dead-end occupation. Only when chatting to a regular customer with whom I had become very friendly was I alerted to this fact. Had I had a man at home to guide me I am sure that I would have been made aware of the situation earlier. As it turned out I was saved just in time, and I am eternally grateful to that particular customer. He convinced me that I was worth better things. So with better things in mind I decided that a radical change was called for.

Memories of my grandfather were never very far from my mind. He was a skilled engineering worker in his day and he was my only role model. Engineering was my first thought when I left school and I had tried hard to find myself a job in that industry; now it was a must. Mother, who was a member of the Mothers' Union at the local church, mentioned my situation to the priest. So with the help of Mother, Father Bluett and God Himself, I was suitably installed in a local engineering company, Kingston Engineering. Local it was too – just fifteen minutes walk from home. I was happy.

In my ignorance I was under the impression that I had been

taken on as an apprentice – after all, I was receiving an apprentice's wage. I was totally unaware of the restrictive practices of the trade union. It was only when I was told that I *had* to join the union that it was made clear to me that I could not become an apprentice because at the grand old age of seventeen I was *too old*. Therefore, for the rest of my life I would never be recognised as a skilled tradesman, regardless of my capabilities. I was given a small pay rise with no compensating back pay, and that was that.

I have avoided dwelling too much on the disadvantages of being brought up without the guidance of a father. I could not believe, though, that because of that I was condemned to the status of the unskilled or, at best, semi-skilled. It seemed so cruel. Little wonder then that I took a very strong dislike to unions for the rest of my life! To say that I was bitter is an understatement. I made up my mind there and then that I would never succumb to the mindless power of the unions. I was determined to gain as much skill as I could and take it from there.

Eventually the war came along, and – surprise, surprise! – I found myself in a reserved occupation. This meant I could not be called to serve in the forces, although after many attempts I did get into the RAF Volunteer Reserve. The delay, however, probably saved my life. That's fate, if you like.

The intervention of the war did in fact change my status. Union power was now practically non-existent. Now I was allowed to do any job for which I was suited, and I took advantage of the situation. The union, not to be outdone, had to have their

Me at nineteen, 1940.

little dig. Well, it was more of a big dig. Although I could now be assigned to do any job, and although I could do most better than many (forgive the lack of modesty), I was to be given the title of 'Dilute' – a sneaky device to prevent me and others in similar circumstances from using our skills if we survived the war. Well, I am delighted to say that the sneaky device did not work.

As the war dragged on it very soon went from bad to worse. Hull, constantly referred to on the news as an East Coast town, suffered more than most from the continued bombing, and we, like so many others, were caught up in the devastation. On four separate occasions our house was so severely damaged that we had to be evacuated for some considerable time.

My sister, Mary, and her two very small children were living with us as her husband, Arthur, was doing his bit in North Africa. The air-raid shelter, which was in the garden very close to the house, was where we spent many, many hours. The nights when we were made homeless were particularly stressful. There were Mother, Mary and her two little ones, Ada and I, all cramped together with no heat of any kind for hours on end. My brother, Harry, was already a prisoner of war. I was not the only one who grew up quickly in those days.

My sister, Mary, 1940.

Mary's two little ones.

For the three nights of the Blitz – three nights of intense bombing – I was working on the night shift at Kingston Engineering, which, as I have said, was only a few minutes' walk from where we lived. On those three nights we were very lucky. Our works were right in the thick of it. Reckitts, a well-known and old-established company just a few metres down the street, was completely destroyed. In fact, the street, Dansom Lane, was alight from one end to the other. Just behind our works the gas company, along with its gasometer, was blown up, as was the bank at the corner of the street. A large piece of stone along with other debris from the bank thundered down through the roof on to the escape hatch of our shelter. Thankfully, there were no injuries. The following morning the devastation was such that it took me a little over an hour to get back home, and that was on my motorcycle. In truth I experienced more action living in Hull than I did during my eventual time in the RAF. Only those who lived through it can know the full extent of the trauma. I have never met anyone from any other part of the country who knows that Hull suffered from the attentions of the doodlebug (the V-1 rocket). People still doubt the truth of this statement.

The threat of invasion was ever present and a small group of us volunteered to stay behind in such an event. Known as the Demolition Squad, our job was to break up every piece of equipment (machinery and the like), set fire to the buildings and do as much damage as was possible. Thank goodness this situation never materialised!

Alan Williamson describes the Demolition Squads in his book *East Ridings Secret Resistance*: 'Invariably they would be well known to each other and with similar employment. Although they were required to sign the Official Secrets Act, they were not enrolled in either the regular forces or the Home Guard. They were in effect private citizens, who if caught during their guerrilla activities, would not have the protection of the Geneva Convention, and were more than likely to be shot.' In recent years the Demolition Squads have become known as the Secret Army.

Looking back, I realise that even at the very height of the bombing, with the deafening noise of the anti-aircraft guns, with shrapnel falling all around, I never once felt the slightest bit afraid. I suppose all young men felt that way. My brother and my brother-in-law, along with many of my friends, were in uniform. Sadly some had already lost their lives. I really felt out of it and very uncomfortable. It never crossed my mind that any of the lads who were out there doing their bit would have gladly changed places with me.

My attempts to get into the services had all been in vain. The army, the air force, the navy, the merchant navy – all had been tried. I was stuck in a reserved occupation – a supposedly very important job – and I was now getting on with my life, in a rut, working on the day shift for a week, working on the night shift for a week. Life was getting tedious.

Then I met an angel. In 1943 (10 July, to be exact) Ivy and I were married. Our wedding took place on the Saturday, and our honeymoon lasted all the next day, Sunday. On Monday we were back at work.

Clothes, along with almost everything else, were on ration.

E. Fullerton.

THE KINGSTON ENGINEERING COMPANY LIMITED,

DANSOM LANE,

HULL.

The Directors express their sincere thanks to those
who have volunteered to come in and assist in case
of invasion.

Your duty will be to report to the Works immediately
to hear the ringing of church bells and wait for
orders.

Instructions may be given by Mr. H. Morris,
Mr. R. Markham, Mr. F. Markham or Mr. T. Simpkins,
or any other official who has been given previous
instructions.

P.S.- If any circumstances have arisen which may
prevent you from fulfilling this duty, please
report to Mr. F. Markham at once.

FRM/RSB.

KINGSTON ENGINEERING Co. LTD.

_____ DIRECTOR

THE MILITARY AUTHORITIES HAVE REQUESTED
A REHEARSAL FOR TOMORROW (THURSDAY)
EVENING AT 7 pm AND YOU MUST ATTEND THESE
WORKS AT THAT TIME.

The Demolition Squad at Kingston Engineering.

For the wedding I was in need of a new suit, but the only suit one could buy (provided one had enough clothing coupons) was what was known as a utility suit. Indeed, everything one bought new was a utility something or other. The utility suit was a suit made with the smallest amount of cloth. In consequence it had drainpipe trousers – quite popular these days, but way back then they were not something to be found dead in let alone to be wed in. To avoid embarrassment, the local tailor suggested what seemed at the time to be a crafty manoeuvre. He advised me to purchase a suit that was several sizes too big. This was no difficult task considering my stature, or lack of it. The bright idea was to butcher (I use that word purposely) the utility suit and remake it using the abundance of material so acquired. Sad to say, though not surprisingly, it did not work out too successfully, as the wedding photographs testify, but I was stuck with it.

Our wedding, 1943.

We scraped together a few more clothing coupons for Ivy's wedding dress, which was also blighted by the dreaded utility label. In an endeavour to make the dress more fitting for the occasion I dismantled a diamanté (I think that's the right name) necklace and fitted the stones on to a strip of white satin, which the dressmaker sewed around the neckline of the dress. Although I say it myself, it looked a real treat. My dear wife-to-be, God bless her, thought I was Mr Wonderful!

We had a single-tier wedding cake courtesy of various members of the family, who contributed some of their food coupons. However, in spite of their sacrifice, the cake was a very plain cake, with little fruit and none of the customary icing. Nevertheless the cake did look the part, hiding as it did under a cardboard cover decorated in a suitable fashion, with plaster of Paris masquerading as icing sugar. This piece of deception was on hire from the shop where the cake was purchased, and had to be returned for further use.

In November 1941 I had been allowed to join the R A F Volunteer Reserve. This had come about because the air force at that time was getting desperately short of aircrew. It was decreed that anyone in a reserved occupation would be allowed to join provided they volunteered for aircrew duties. The upshot of this was that I went down to Cardington for four days, passed the selection board, and was put on four months' deferred service. I was now about to become a flyer.

1941

All communications should be addressed to the
Officer-in-Charge.

From OFFICER-IN-CHARGE,
ROYAL AIR FORCE SECTION,
COMBINED RECRUITING CENTRE, JAMESON - STREET
To. E. Fullerton   HULL.

Date :

THIS LETTER SHOULD BE SHOWN ON ARRIVAL AT THE RECRUITING CENTRE.

SIR,
With reference to your application for enlistment into the Royal Air Force Volunteer Reserve, it is requested that you will report at this Centre on....8 - 10 - 41....as soon after 9 a.m. as possible. at 10, A M
2. The vacancy for which you are being considered is that of....A.C.H....u/t....aircrew
3. You will be required to proceed to a Recruits' Centre for all station.

Translation A C u u/t aircrew =
Aircraftsman grade 2 under training Aircrew

RAF recruitment form.

So now, in the middle of 1943, how come I was still in Civvy Street? Well, it happened like this:

On returning to my job at Kingston Engineering, my boss was not at all pleased (in fact, he was quite peeved) when I told him I was destined to serve His Majesty King George. So much so, in fact, that he sacked me on the spot! Well, I had no idea that he cared, and so I felt quite wanted. In fact, I could have kissed him! I now felt free and elated!

My elation was deemed to be short-lived, however. On reporting to the labour exchange, as was the directive during the war years, I was directed to C. D. Holmes (now non-existent), a company which was making triple-expansion engines for minesweepers. I explained to the manager that I was due to go into the air force, but that I would be a good lad and serve them well until my enlistment. The manager said, "Start tomorrow." I did, and all seemed well.

About two weeks after joining the company, the boss, during one of his inspection tours, made his way over to me to have what I thought was to be a friendly chat.

"You're the young fella who's going into the air force, aren't you?"

"That's right," I beamed.

"Well, you are working for the Admiralty now, so you can forget about that."

Talk about out of the frying pan into the fire! It was my turn to be peeved, and I was!

It turned out that there was another young chap who was in a similar position. This young chap was hell-bent on getting into the merchant navy and did not take kindly to being bamboozled by the boss, whom he did not love very much. Positive action was the order of the day, declared my new-found ally, so together we went on strike – well, more of a go-slow really. Now, this was positive action all right – positively dangerous and downright stupid, considering there were only the two of us and the whole bloody nation was at war. Nevertheless we persisted, and although it took many months we were both released at the same time. To cut a long story short, we found out that the boss was convinced that we would both finish up in the army, and therefore conceded defeat. We were lucky!

My life in the 'mob' was on the whole pretty uneventful – except, that is, for a serious vehicle accident which left me with a fractured spine and almost finished me off. It seemed I was never destined to be a flyer. Eventually I was shipped off to India as an engine fitter.

India
1944–7

Early morning.

Engine testing.

India was not, in my opinion, the best place to spend three years, although the threat of invasion of that hot, smelly country by the Japanese was now history. The war with Japan was, however, far from over. Indeed, we out there were convinced that this conflict would continue for many more years. Fortunately, just as we were about to be shipped further east, the atomic bomb made its dramatic and devastating appearance.

The word 'fortunately' as I have just used it may cause the reader to think that I condone, or perhaps look very lightly on, the wholesale loss of life and abject suffering caused by this historic event. I believe, however, as I think most people believe, that it actually saved more lives and prevented more suffering than it caused. So I say that the news of its coming brought us nothing but relief and hope where there was very little before.

The war in Europe finished, as we all know, in 1945. It was April 1947 before I was shipped home, and I often wonder just how much longer we would have remained, running what amounted to a civil air service, if it had not been for the fact that a large part of the air force went on strike – an event one will not find a mention of in the history books. As it happened I was not involved, as I along with just two other dogsbodies were – would you believe it? – on our own, running what was known as a staging post. When we eventually arrived home the war was almost forgotten and so were we.

Now the war was over, the union began flexing its muscles. The fight for my future was just beginning. I was determined to earn a crust as a skilled worker, and everyone else, it seemed, was determined to stop me. What a pathetic lot some of these union men seemed! The less skill they possessed, the more active they were in the union. Every time I landed a skilled job, some devoted trade-union man would gleefully try to get me sacked, or, failing that, would endeavour to have me reduced to a semi-skilled position with a subsequent reduction in pay. Whenever this occurred I simply upped sticks and left, with the result that I had thirteen jobs before I eventually became my own boss.

CHAPTER 4

The last job I had prior to starting my own little business was with a small firm of toolmakers, the boss of which was a man with a similar background to mine. He also refused to kowtow to the unions, and was in consequence very successful. The word 'toolmaking' can be a little misleading to anyone not familiar with engineering. It doesn't refer to the familiar hand tools as used by craftsmen, but to special pieces of machinery or measuring equipment, designed for very specific functions. Toolmaking therefore demands the highest skill, calling for greater accuracy than in most other types of engineering. I was quite happy in this employment and became the highest-paid man on the payroll – apart from the general manager, that is. In spite of this, I was, as always, constantly planning to do my own thing. It must be said, however, that this job, along with the many changes of employment I had been forced to make, courtesy of the dedicated union officials, gave me a wealth of valuable experience which, as it turned out, served me very well throughout the following years.

During these changes of employment I worked as chief engineer at what was then Clover Dairies, and later in a similar capacity at a local bakery. These two appointments turned out to be perhaps the most useful of all. The hygiene requirements in the food industry, along with the need for more and better methods of production, remained uppermost in my thoughts all through the intervening years, until I eventually found myself in a position to do something about it. When that time finally came I knew that I would be successful, although I never thought for one moment that I would establish not one but two companies, with turnovers of more than £3.5 million each (in those days that was a lot of loot), along with exports to more than twenty-five countries!

The toolmaking job was the last time I ever worked for someone else. It was straight from there that I made my first tentative steps to self-employment. The road to this end was painfully long, poverty-stricken, and frustrating beyond belief. Many were the times I almost gave up and went back to my old job – in fact, I did this at one time. My old boss took me back at a reduced salary, but, much to his surprise, I returned to have another go and eventually succeeded.

You see, I had no money – not a bean. I had no savings whatsoever. My weekly wage, though, was a little above the average for a tradesman.

Now, just to put the matter straight before proceeding further, I did not care very much for my wife's Christian name, though I did care for her very, very much. Ivy disliked her name also – in fact, very, very much. We decided therefore that her name was to be Irene – a name we both liked very, very, very much. From now on when I speak of Irene the reader will know that I am speaking about the dearest and sweetest angel that ever entered a man's life; and I miss her so.

Dearest Irene.

Irene and I were struggling to make ends meet while buying things for the home. I was working as much overtime as I could get, seven days a week and many late nights, still nurturing my dream, which seemed as distant as ever. Everything we bought was on the never-never, as hire purchase was then known. There were no credit cards in those days. We made all our purchases through what was known as a club agent. The agent issued us with a cheque, the amount of which was negotiated according to our creditworthiness, and the amount of the weekly payments was specified.

Christmas was the most difficult time. Having planned to spend a specific amount on presents for those nearest to us, we would inadvertently overspend our budget. The payments usually lasted until the same time the following year, when it all started again. I was always thoroughly ashamed of having to rely on the 'club man', as the credit agent was then known – not least because he added a hefty sixteen per cent or so to the purchase price. But try as we did, we never seemed to be able to accumulate enough savings to be in a position to pay cash for our purchases. Yes, we were living from hand to mouth in those so-called good old days.

This was at a time when Irene's health was not at its best. For the second time she suffered the loss of a stillborn child, having lost our firstborn during my time in the air force. When we discovered that she was pregnant for the third time I decided – or rather *we* decided – that we would consult a doctor privately. I still don't know where we found the money for this, but we did and I am pleased to say that it paid off. We were blessed with Margaret, our third and only child, and she is a treasure. With the help of her lovely young husband, Charles Mackay, they have produced our only grandchild, Richard Fullerton Mackay, of whom I am immensely proud.

Margaret, Charles and Richard.

The first house we occupied was a rented one, the address of this abode being May Villas, Haddon Street, Hawthorn Avenue, Hull. It consisted of a living room and a tiny kitchenette on the ground floor, and two small bedrooms – a two-up two-down, as they were known at the time. There was an outside loo in the backyard, which was too small to swing a cat in. The period between our marriage and my enlistment in HM Forces was something like six months, during which time we had very little time to accumulate a substantial amount of furniture or the other chattels which go to make up a home. Everything was still on ration, and was blighted by the utility label. It was also expensive. In consequence, our total purchases consisted of a second-hand bed, a second-hand wardrobe, a table and two chairs of similar vintage, and an old deckchair which served as a recliner or easy chair, and which we took turns in using. We had no proper floor coverings, the bedroom and the living-room floors being covered with random pieces of canvas, which were like roofing felt with one shiny side. These pieces of canvas were all of different colours and design, but when nailed to the floor and painted all the same colour (using a special paint known as Treadonit) they looked at least clean and reasonably tidy. To complete the picture an old blanket provided the semblance of a carpet. That was our home at the beginning of our married life.

On returning home after the war, the years were fairly humdrum. We never went anywhere, or really did anything, from one year's end to another. In pursuit of my dream we moved into a rented house which had a large garden at the rear. This allowed me to build some sort of workshop, which I hoped would lead me to my ultimate dream. With this aim in mind, I was working every bit of overtime that I could get, and in addition I worked until the early hours of the mornings improving the house. We were very happy!

By now I was in receipt of a substantial wage – that is, by the standards prevailing. Nevertheless, because of my commitment to starting my own business, I was considered just a dreamer. Our house, the house with the large garden, the house which was to launch me on my way to riches, was a tip. It was unbelievable. The first day we moved in, a cat moved in with us. It made its appearance, when all the doors and windows were closed, by simply walking under the front door by way of a very worn step! Replacing the step was the first of the many tasks which needed my attention and which kept me out of mischief for some four years or more.

It was just after we had moved into this house in Hawthorn Avenue that a stroke of luck came my way. Apparently the house had quite recently been inherited, and the new owners were ready and willing to sell. The asking price was £250 – not a very large sum of money, even in those days – but in our hard-up state we were not too optimistic that we would be able to raise the money. Surprise, however, followed surprise. I plucked up the courage to apply for a mortgage and, with little ado, we became property owners. I now had an asset, would you believe! It was turning this asset into something better that took me so long. Nevertheless, it was this seemingly small change of circumstances that put me on the first rung of the ladder to success.

It is only on reflection and with hindsight that I can see the size of the task I had set myself. In fact, I still view with some wonderment how much energy I had at my disposal when I was young. In addition to replacing the previously mentioned worn step at the front door, the staircase needed to be completely rebuilt and the ceiling over the stairs had collapsed, leaving a gaping hole. There was also a strong smell of gas, which I eventually traced to a nail which had been driven through a lead gas pipe in the kitchen wall.

Adjacent to the kitchen was a walk-in pantry. The one window in this quite spacious pantry was very small and could not be opened. Consequently the whole room smelt very damp and fusty. It was also very dark. To top the lot it was home to those little furry creatures – mice. There were so many major defects that it is difficult to say which were the worst! One room, which in its day had been quite something, had large French windows opening out to the long garden, except the doors could no longer be opened as they were literally falling apart. The floor in this once elegant room was fully seven inches (eighteen centimetres) lower at one end than the rest of the floor. In fact, the skirting board looked more like a dado rail it was so far up the wall. The subsidence responsible for this state of affairs had affected many other parts of the house. The French windows, for instance, in addition to their dilapidated state, were as lopsided as it is possible to believe – as indeed were other windows in this Walt Disney abode.

Fortunately the worst of the problems were at the rear of the house. The front was remarkably presentable – that is apart from the fact that the two windows in the front were in dire need of replacement. At the rear the foundations had sunk beneath ground level, along with the damp course; consequently rising damp was well established and flourishing. This was undoubtedly my biggest worry. If I could not rectify the rising damp, then this promising asset would turn out to be a real liability. Putting right this menacing hazard was both dangerous and time-consuming, and I was therefore greatly relieved when I had completed it satisfactorily. My visions of the whole house collapsing round my ears thankfully never materialised.

Having cured the damp problem I knew that I could cope with the remaining tasks, in spite of their numbers. The biggest of the remaining problems was the sloping floor, so I set to work removing the floorboards adjacent to the walls, removing the skirting boards and sawing through all the joists after first building many brick pillars to support the floor in its new position. Replacing the floorboards and the skirting boards and making good the plasterwork was then pretty elementary, though time-consuming. All this had to be done in the evenings and at weekends.

The brick joist supports consumed a large number of bricks, which under normal circumstances would have further stretched my meagre finances. However, I had unknowingly bought a virtual brick mine. The garden, which was more like a jungle, having been sadly neglected along with the house, was laced from one end to the other with wide paths made entirely of old bricks salvaged from the demolition of numerous air-raid shelters. I was very pleased with this situation, in spite of the fact that the task of digging up and cleaning my inheritance was a long and tedious one.

As I tackled each and every one of the never-ending jobs as they came along, my dream of building a workshop seemed to be as far distant as ever, but I pressed on. It must be said, however, that this unexpected bonus of bricks galore tempered my impatience as I realised that the project – the ever elusive project – could be built of brick with no monetary cost. How could I not feel grateful?

Eventually the house repairs came to an end and I was able to concentrate on my dream. I was a little older, but all the repairs had been done. The French windows had been replaced, the sloping floor no longer sloped, the wall separating the front room from the adjoining room had been taken down and the two rooms had become one. Furnished with a serving hatch in the kitchen wall and suitably decorated it took on the title 'lounge'. Although I say it myself, I was very pleased with the result. The room was very spacious, and with the new French windows looking out on to the garden it was very nice. It was a pity about the garden, though – its turn for attention was as yet some time in the future. The mice problem had been completely eliminated, and the smelly pantry had been transformed into a very nice bathroom, with a large window and modern plumbing.

I had built, for the want of a better name, a veranda. This was constructed mainly in brick, by courtesy of my inheritance, the 'brick mine'. With a roof of glass and timber it was both roomy and light, and, best of all, it encompassed what had previously been the outside toilet, adjoining a dirty old coalhouse. It was now a modern inside toilet, and the coalhouse, with newly plastered walls, was a clean and useful store. A door gave easy access to the garden, but, best of all, a further

The workshop door, in the veranda.

door at the end of this structure was to be the entrance to my workshop. The dream was about to become a reality!

Once more I was digging up, cleaning and washing the bricks like there was no tomorrow, and, after the long and painful task of laying the foundations and the concrete floor, the brickwork of my fabulous venture began to grow, course upon course. It was at this late stage that the awful truth of the situation dawned upon me: the non-optional location of this structure sadly restricted the size of my dream. This dream, which had eluded me for so very long, seemed at this stage to be in real jeopardy.

I could see now only too clearly that it would be impossible

Building my first workshop – the one that never was.

to install large machines. Access to the rear of the house was too restricted. I felt devastated. During all the years of planning and hard work I had neglected to look far enough ahead. Now it was necessary for a complete rethink.

The most amazing thing is that what seemed to me to be a complete and utter disaster turned out to be a blessing in disguise. The house had now become a saleable asset. It was with this in mind that I formulated a more ambitious plan. My new plan now, however, depended entirely on how my dear long-suffering wife would view the new situation. After years of living on a virtual building site she had just become accustomed to a more pleasant existence. It was therefore with some trepidation that I explained my new scheme. Without batting an eyelid she readily gave her ungrudging consent – I said she was an angel – and, boy, was I happy!

First things first: we set about having the house valued. The house we had purchased for £250 was now, after much hard work, apparently worth £1,800. By today's standards it does not seem a great deal, but this was in the 1950s. This meant that we could look for alternative accommodation – a place with access to the rear, along with room for a workshop. Further consultation with Irene produced a scheme with even more potential: it was decided that if we could purchase a small shop, provided it also had the other requisite features, this would be ideal. Irene's idea was to manage the shop herself. Hopefully this would subsidise our income during the inevitable lean times which we both anticipated.

Frankly, I was not looking forward to starting all over again, but I had come to terms with it when an unexpected change of circumstances developed. I had been to view a small shop which was up for sale just a short distance from home. Thinking it had more or less all the things I was looking for, I was seriously considering it when, much to my surprise, the man who was selling the property advised me against doing so. I had briefly explained to him my plans for the future, and now this complete stranger was advising me that buying it would be a mistake. He went on to explain that he did not think the income from the shop would be sufficient for our needs, etc., etc. I was quite impressed by the honesty of this tall, good-looking, pleasant young man, and that was the beginning of our friendship with Harold and his pretty wife. I had reason many years later to look back on this with a slightly different view; although our friendship lasted many pleasant years, I later had reason to question my first assessment of the man.

The unexpected change of circumstances, to which I referred

earlier, came by way of a telephone call from Harold a couple of days after our first meeting.

"Have you considered taking a partner?" were almost the first words he uttered.

"I have," I replied, and without going into much detail I explained why such a situation had not materialised. In answer to his further request, I agreed to talk to him about going into partnership together, and a meeting was arranged. The rethinking now started again. His was an offer I just had to think about. It could save me the task of moving house. Whether it was the thought of this, along with the thought of the long, hard slog I was already contemplating, or the thought of the £1,000 this man was offering me for a part of the action, I don't really know, but I made the big decision.

It must be said at this point, I was not planning on creating a large engineering works; a small engineering workshop with perhaps six or seven employees was the extent of my ambitions. With the injection of such a large sum, and taking on a partner, I decided that I should plan for a business twice the size. This did not seem to me to be too outrageous – after all, this man claimed to have bookkeeping knowledge which would be useful – and so plans accordingly were made.

One thousand pounds! That was ten hundred pounds – ten hundred! I had never had even £100 in all my life! The very thought of it frightened me. Perhaps that was why I decided to accept just £600, in return for which I agreed to give him fifty per cent of my non-existent company. A simple letter of agreement was made and signed by both parties; no solicitor was ever consulted.

That is how the situation remained until a lifetime later. Then, after success which surpassed my wildest dreams, my partner's attitude changed. He became more and more difficult. It was then I decided to end the partnership, by selling the company and giving him exactly half the proceeds. That, as I have said, came a whole lifetime later – a lifetime of which I have little or no regrets; indeed it is one I would gladly live all over again. More about that later.

This new-found wealth remained in the bank untouched while we set about looking for small rented premises. My new friend and partner found the answer to this: a two-storey warehouse, much too large for our modest requirements, with a rent of £4 10s per week. At first I was reluctant to move into this place. It was four or more times the size we needed, with a rent to match.

It was then that fate took a hand. The owners of the property, Messrs Ferriby and Hare, who I feel took pity on us, agreed to rent us just the lower part of this two-storey warehouse at a knock-down rent of thirty shillings a week. Believe it or not, even this was a bit too high for the likes of us. The situation was, I am glad to say, saved by Harold. Harold had a friend who wanted to rent a small workshop for car repairs. He agreed to share the rent, and the space was thus divided equally. We could now afford to pay the rent out of our weekly wages, leaving our small capital intact. This situation prevailed for the next two years or more – the time it took me to organise the workplace in the evenings and at weekends. It was truly a labour of love, and in spite of the time involved I enjoyed every minute of it.

Our first premises. The warehouse is at the right in the rear.

Converting the warehouse into a workshop, as I have said, took more than two years. This was due in the main to my determination to make the bank balance last. It was also because the premises were in a state consistent with years of neglect. The cleaning of the place alone was a dirty, thankless task, taking up much valuable time. The remains of a cat which had lost its meow months previously did not help the situation either. Its prevailing perfume did indeed prevail, over and above the aroma of the fertiliser which had been the main occupant. All in all, a really unwelcome treat for the nostrils! But we did get it cheap! By far the most difficult, most time-consuming task was the reorganising of the electrical installation. It consisted of only four old lights and a number of antique three-pin sockets, all single phase. There was no three-phase wiring at all, which was a must for our purpose. I had not expected this problem and I was suddenly plunged into despair. The possibility of a very costly exercise presented itself. What was I to do?

In an endeavour to reduce the costs to a minimum, I set to work, taking down and dismantling the whole of this ancient paraphernalia. My plan was to use as much of the reclaimed bits and pieces as possible. Well, it transpired that the wire itself was quite sound, and, surprisingly, there was a lot of it. Furthermore the installation (being of the vintage type, as I have said) consisted of steel tubing – conduit, as it was known then. Now this tubing along with some of the fittings could be used again. The tubing was screwed at each end and was of random lengths, but once again there was lots of it. There had to be a snag, however! Although I could cut the tubing to any length, I would not be able to replace the screwed portion, which was required to join the tubes or fittings together. That required tools I did not have. There was only one thing for it: by careful selection of different lengths of conduit, I was able to rearrange all the wiring with the outlets more or less in the positions that were required. It was time-consuming, but it was interesting – like doing a giant jigsaw puzzle. In the end, I completed the whole of the wiring without spending a penny! I felt I was making some progress. I continued to work whenever the opportunity presented itself: evenings, weekends and all holidays. Frankly, I was never in the house. Irene, as I remember, never once complained. Bless her!

The time eventually came when I was able to buy an old lathe – a very old lathe (it had first seen the light of day around 1930) – and a small milling machine of similar vintage. They both came from a local scrap merchant along with various other bits and pieces. These machines needed to be driven by belts from cumbersome pulleys, with shafts and brackets, all of which had to be fixed to the ceiling. I found this to be a difficult and tiresome job, working on my own most of the time with little or no help. A massive old-fashioned twelve-horsepower electric motor, purchased from the same scrap merchant, completed this somewhat hotchpotch installation. The electrical starter for this ancient motor was given to me by a sympathetic friendly electrician, thereby saving me a sizeable slice of the bank balance. I will always be very grateful to him, along with a few others who gave me help and encouragement at a time when I needed both in considerable measure!

Discarded equipment (other people's throw-outs) was destined to be my only source of machinery for the next twenty-odd years. I well remember the red-letter day when I first purchased a *new* machine. For many years I had been accumulating hand tools and measuring equipment, with the result that I was fairly well equipped in that respect. So now

Still getting my hands dirty.

with the lathe, a milling machine and one or two smaller bits and pieces in place, I was ready to begin my search for customers.

Well, there was no way I could look for customers in the evenings or at weekends. To make matters worse I had no transport, or should I say no *suitable* transport! It is true I was the proud owner of a tiny motorcycle. I had bought this a couple of years previously for the princely sum of £25. It was on its last legs then – barely roadworthy! It was certainly not the kind of transport to inspire confidence! There was, however, no alternative. I would have to give up my job and sally forth on my trusty steed, the motorcycle. It was my intention to seek work during the daytime, and then carry out the work thus obtained in the evenings. What could be easier? I was oblivious to the scale of the task that I had set myself; so I went once more into the unknown armed with nothing more than blind enthusiasm!

In the land of big, big motor cars and elegant, posh offices, the pampered inhabitants are not accustomed to being accosted by the likes of yours truly – a self-made, self-contained entrepreneur – especially if he turns up soaking wet, with a soggy briefcase (empty, by the way) dripping water all over the wall-to-wall carpets! Well, having the great gift of foresight, I realised this from the very outset, would you believe! In fact, I had my master stroke worked out. I would enter the holy of holies just like any other of the poor unfortunates who made their living touting for business. (Poor unfortunates indeed! With company car, etc., and unbridled pomposity they presented formidable competition!) However, nothing ventured, nothing gained! I would arrive at my planned location, select a spot out of sight and earshot of my unsuspecting target, remove the plastic bags and elastic bands from my feet and legs, remove also the waterproof cape, place them in the box I had made for them, take out my empty briefcase and complete the change from the dripping-wet caterpillar into the elegant butterfly of my imagination!

Thus transformed I would saunter, with all the nonchalance I could muster, to the lovely snooty young lady cocooned in the tranquillity of her sumptuous surroundings. It is then that I would play my master stroke: taking out my business card emblazoned with the words 'TURBO TOOLS, Tool Makers', I would present it to her just like my aforementioned competitors. How's that?

Six years or more had passed since I chose that name for my – ahem – company. I feel sure that I was the first ever to use the name 'Turbo' as a company name, though through the years it has become quite commonplace. The name was synonymous with the work I was doing at the time: namely, making specialised tools for the manufacture of turbine blades for the engines of the relatively new and up-and-coming jet aircraft. It was my success in this particular field of up-to-date technology which prompted me to adopt this name. I was somewhat proud of this work I was doing for Rolls-Royce Engines, particularly because my efforts came to the notice of the bigwigs at Rolls-Royce, who decided to send no less than six members of their top team to visit the company where I was employed! Dare I say it, the object of their visit was to see how we had achieved such accuracy! I say 'we' because the works manager, Alan Farmer (a man for whom I always had a great admiration), and I were jointly responsible for a product which seemingly surprised everyone at Rolls-Royce. That's enough bragging, methinks, for the moment.

This looking for work did not come easily, mainly because of my lack of better transport. I remember spending the whole of one day travelling on foot throughout the industrial area of Leeds. I must have covered many miles, all to no avail, without a glimpse or a promise of work. At one point I was on the very verge of giving up completely! With our meagre capital diminishing at an alarming rate, there seemed nothing left except to go cap in hand back to my old employer and ask to be reinstated – on a purely temporary basis, of course. With a knowing smile on his face, he readily agreed – but at a reduced salary, of course.

Frankly, I cannot recall just how or when I made the breakthrough which allowed me finally to give up my job and return to have another go, but it did happen and I survived. By this time, however, I had sold as many of our possessions as I could, bearing in mind that we had but a few. I had also, from the very outset, reduced my take-home pay to a bare minimum.

We had been literally living from hand to mouth for a full three years or more. Things had become very difficult indeed, but just as I was beginning to think seriously about failure I discovered that I was holding my own. I began to make progress. I was still working on my own, but doing numerous small maintenance jobs – mainly for smaller companies, but the odd job for better-established companies. The formula (looking for work during the day and doing the work so gained by night and weekends) was beginning to pay off. When I think of the many, many hours, the long days, and the years without holidays, I marvel at the energy I possessed during those days. I must say, though, that I have never felt happier.

Once I had passed the break-even point, as it were, things went from strength to strength, albeit slowly. At this time Irene joined me at the works, taking an active part in the making of a millionaire.

This was a very happy time for us both. No longer was Irene alone in the house for hours on end; nor was I working alone. The small tasks Irene performed were out of all proportion to the help her presence gave me. By answering the telephone, she allowed me to continue with whatever job I had in hand. My production improved no end and I began to taste success.

Irene, who had no previous experience of typing, became very proficient at the one-finger-typing routine. In no time at all she was typing my letters, making out invoices and, most importantly, correcting my spelling – which I have to say is by any standard appalling. For many months Irene continued to do her bit free, gratis, which suited the financial situation. Eventually I was able to pay her the handsome amount of £3 per week, which also suited our financial situation. In fact, we were in some danger of becoming rich all of a sudden.

As I mentioned earlier, Harold had at our first meeting told me that along with the money he had had to invest, he also had bookkeeping experience which he felt would be of value to our venture. It turned out that the bookkeeping experience was that of a corner shopkeeper – not quite what I had expected. I soon discovered that he had no special skills to speak of, but he seemed to be a likeable lad. I had committed myself to an equal partnership and that was that. Harold's employment was that of a salesman, travelling from corner shop to corner shop selling sweets. This provided him with a small car. Although I did not know the extent of his salary, he seemed quite comfortably off. He also had a passion for football and played in a local amateur team. Consequently in the earlier days, when I was working all the hours that God sends, Harold was unfortunately often unavailable when I really could have done with some help.

It therefore came as a bit of a surprise – well, more of a shock – when one day he suddenly suggested that he joined me in what at that time was no more than a one-man band. There was absolutely nothing he could do which would have been useful. Choosing my words carefully, I endeavoured to explain the situation as I saw it. In sheer desperation I made the suggestion that perhaps he could apply for a job as a semi-skilled worker at one of the local engineering companies where I was not unknown. Desperation, it seems, at times pays off, and this is just what happened. While Harold was gaining a little experience I took on my first apprentice. Now I was not just an up-and-coming entrepreneur; I was now an employer!

Progress continued, be it at times a little slow! Harold did join in the fun, and little by little we increased our staff, employing (much to his surprise) a semi-skilled friend to whom I had promised a job several years earlier. Norman Goodison was his name.

Norman was a real character. His skills were somewhat suspect, but his loyalty was beyond reproach, and a harder worker there never was! Later I shall relate some of the capers our Norman was involved in. There never existed an employer-and-employee relationship between Norman and me, and we remained firm friends to the end. There were times, however, when he exasperated me beyond all endurance. He was the only man who could make me lose my cool. No doubt this was one of his finest achievements – he did it constantly!

Other members of staff over the years were often heard to say, "There go Ted and Norman – at it again."

Throughout the whole of my working life I refused to be called Mr Fullerton; it was always Ted. The common bond between Ted and staff produced a workforce of extraordinary loyalty, for which I am eternally grateful and immensely proud.

This might be a good time just to squeeze in one of Norman's capers: Norman is the only person I know of who actually passed his driving test with neither boots nor shoes on his feet. How did our Norman persuade the examiner to let him remove his boots for the test? Perhaps he persuaded the examiner to remove his footwear at the same time! Who knows? The driving test and the driving lessons were paid for by the company – simply a part of my plan to find my friend a useful occupation, keep him out of my hair and save my sanity! As it turned out, Norman became a good, reliable driver, doing a useful job until his retirement. God bless him! Come to think of it, my sanity prevailed.

Irene's contribution increased in usefulness as did the small wage we were able to pay her. More importantly, she was no longer spending countless hours on her own and was enjoying the work. I was able to find useful work for Harold, and the general feeling was one of optimism as work opportunities continued to increase.

Irene, as I have mentioned, had no previous experience of typing. She had, however, been in charge of the Complaints Department at a local laundry (not the most envious of positions). She was therefore not unaccustomed to dealing with people and making important decisions. This no doubt helped

Irene and me at her first piano.

her to settle down so well to office routine. Having said all that, I must add that she was not without talent; in fact, she was a very accomplished pianist. Her talent at the keyboard was very much admired by all who heard her play. She was, though, very introvert. She hated attention and would not readily play for strangers. If she ever suspected that anyone was about to record her playing she simply stopped. I bitterly regret that I was never able to persuade her to change her mind regarding this. I do think her exceptional talent deserved to be recorded.

Irene had not always been quite so introvert. Indeed, in our courting days she would play almost anywhere, and at any time. I clearly remember during the war Irene, myself and a friend of mine spending many happy hours in the local pub. It was customary in those days for everyone to sing, as almost every pub had a piano. Those that did not usually had someone with a piano accordion, or at least a mouth organ. It really was Merrie England in those days. I well remember, as one walked along the streets around eight o'clock each evening, every pub one passed echoed to the sound of people singing. There were very few alcohol-induced fights in those days. People were too busy singing – singing and fighting do not go together, you see! What a pity that the town council of later years did not consider this when, in their infinite wisdom, they banned singing in pubs unless they were specifically licensed for it. That put an end to the pubs as we of our generation knew them – a sad thing, I think. Irene would be easily persuaded to tinkle the ivories in the pub for the enjoyment of all, although she was not one for drinking. The pub's customers, however, were not always aware of that situation, and at frequent intervals would be kind enough to send a drink or two over in appreciation of her talents. Well, Cyril (my friend) and I, were quite good at it – the drinking bit, I mean! In consequence we usually had a good time at little cost to ourselves, thanks to dearest Irene. All of this happened before my eventual enlistment and subsequent passage to India. It was, I am sure, during my absence, especially at the time that Irene suffered the loss of our first stillborn child, that she began to develop a mild form of agoraphobia. After my return to Civvy Street, matters were made much worse by the loss of our second child to the same cause. In my endeavour to achieve my long-standing ambition of self-employment, I was blissfully unaware of what was happening to Irene. Long before I was able to start my long slog to betterment, I was working every bit of overtime I could get. It must have been a very lonely time for her, and, alas! it continued for so many years. I am overcome with guilt and remorse as I reflect on the outrageous manner in which I neglected her. For many years we never went out, anywhere, and holidays were never even dreamed of.

As business started to improve, I recognised Irene's problem (which had by now become my problem, and rightly so!), and I was determined to help her overcome it. Perhaps I should mention that at this stage in our lives we could not be considered wealthy. That is to say, there was not a lot of money available for lavish holidays, although our investment was increasing. My priority now was to find something a bit out of the ordinary – something Irene would find impossible to refuse. It was as I was contemplating this that I recalled a programme we had recently watched together on the television (the nine-inch television – real luxury, what?). It was about life on board the *QE2*.

'This is just the thing,' I thought.

It was during my attempts to persuade her to accept this holiday that I realised more fully the depths of her difficulties. Nevertheless I persisted, and she accepted, reluctantly. It became obvious to me that Irene had accepted my proposals more for my sake than for her own. Indeed, I had talked about cruising on and off throughout the years, though I never thought it would happen. In truth, though, it was not because of my desire to go cruising that I proposed it. It was, I thought, the very thing which would help return Irene to her previous state of good health. I am pleased to say that it did the trick, but I was not to know this until much later. Having acquired her consent, I set about making the arrangements – the booking, etc. I have to admit that in my naivety I thought the price I was quoted for this extravagant holiday was for us both; it transpired that it was in fact only for one, and the total was twice what I had expected.

The period between the booking and the actual sailing was a little difficult. One could be forgiven for thinking that Irene was awaiting admission to hospital, or some such unwelcome event. There were several times when I had serious doubts about going through with our plans, and I almost called them off. Thank goodness I didn't!

The time for our departure arrived, and because of the long drive to Southampton I arranged for us to stay overnight at a hotel. All through the long drive, the stay at the hotel (very pleasant) and the first evening on board – an evening of sumptuous dining, followed by ballroom dancing (something which we always used to enjoy) and a stage show – we spoke very little. I dared not even ask how she felt. I had the impression, though, that she did seem a little more relaxed.

The following morning, I could contain myself no longer and I asked her the question: "What do you think?"

Her reply was short and to the point. As I write this there are real tears in my eyes. This very brief moment in my life is one which remains very clearly in my mind and will do so to the end of my days.

"I'm coming again" was her reply.

This was the very moment when Irene and I started living again!

We became regular sailors on that lovely ship, and consequently received many invitations from both the Captain and his officers. Dining at the Captain's table was offered to us on a number of occasions, but this much sought-after invitation we accepted only once. Irene did not like the attention this caused. I understood her feelings about such things and accepted the situation. There was one particular time when I felt a little disappointed. This was when the BBC was filming an episode of *Keeping Up Appearances* (a very popular series on BBC1). The actress playing Mrs Bucket (pronounced Boo-kay, as Mrs Bucket constantly reminded folk!) and the remainder of the cast were on board, and although we mixed with them and enjoyed their company Irene could not bring herself to accept the invitation to take part as an extra. I consoled myself somewhat by keeping the written invitation to do so.

Irene and friends at her baby grand.

The one time we accepted the invitation to sit at the Captain's table was the time when Captain Jackson was in command. Captain Jackson, as it turned out, was from Grimsby, and as I had spent my early schooldays there we shared a common interest. Irene, I am pleased to say, felt at ease in his company – so much so that she agreed to play the piano for him. Mind you, it was mainly through a remiss remark I made to him regarding her aptitude on that instrument. You see, I always took any opportunity to brag a little about Irene's talent. It was immediately after my short spell of bragging that the Captain informed us that he himself had talent of that particular kind. He further informed us that he had had a grand piano brought on board specifically for his personal use. Alarm bells sounded in my head at that very moment. Long before he had finished speaking, I realised that I had put my foot in it and committed her. But things turned out all right after all, and we enjoyed a very nice evening together.

For the remainder of the three-week voyage we shared his company, both at a cocktail party in his quarters and at other functions on board.

CHAPTER 5

By now things were really looking up – so much so that we decided to splash out on a vehicle. We looked through the local paper and an old van – a cheap, very old van – caught our attention. It was situated in a village some fifteen miles or so west of Hull. The problem was how to get there! Well, I still had my motorcycle, but by now the trusty steed was truly on its last legs. With only me on its back it could barely manage thirty miles an hour, and that was with a strong tailwind, but it had to do.

One fine sunny morning the three of us (Harold, me and the ageing two-wheeled transport) set out to conquer the fifteen miles. I don't recall how long it took us to complete the journey, but I do recall very clearly the hilarity of the onlookers who observed us en route. Perhaps it was the sight of the lightweight driver with the heavyweight pillion passenger whose knees encompassed my body like the arms of an easy chair, or perhaps it was because we were both most of the time smoking cigarettes as we slowly and nonchalantly passed along the streets. But we arrived in the end, made our purchase and returned in style with the friendly motorcycle tucked away inside the van!

An old van to most people is just an old van. To me this latest addition to our assets was another small but very important landmark in the pauper's progress. Hitherto collecting supplies and materials had been a real pain in the neck – not to mention the time-consuming element. The little motorcycle was of little use when it came to transporting pieces of metal and the like, so to help me with this task I had purchased an old discarded errand boy's bicycle. This museum piece was of sturdy construction with a metal frame on the front – originally to accommodate a large basket, long since defunct.

With a large box in place of the departed basket, and hooks fitted at various points along the frame, I was able to carry lengths of steel. The box took care of the small bulky bits and pieces. I managed like this for many months, though there were times when I was so loaded that I had to push the bicycle along – a lot less dangerous than trying to ride it. I always carried a hacksaw to cut the steel bars to a suitable length to make this possible. Even with the bars cut to suitable lengths I often felt like a Bengal Lancer. With the coming of the van all this changed for the better and I was really chuffed!

As a precision engineer I was expected to be precise. However, this is where my bad spelling spoiled my image somewhat! My first apprentice, in a spirit of goodwill, suggested that as the bicycle had a very large nameplate fitted under the crossbar, we should have our name along with our occupation emblazoned thereon.

'What a good idea!' thought I.

The lad seemed to be a dab hand with the old paintbrush, so with my blessing he did the deed! On completion it looked to me very stylish – almost professional, in fact. That was because his spelling was akin to mine. He and I had been riding and pushing this contraption all over the city right up until the time we acquired the van, advertising our shortcomings. What price precision? Precision was the very word my artist had misspelt.

Time marched on, and with the march of time we went from strength to strength. In the main we were doing what could be described as the overspill work of the well-established companies in the city. In the beginning J. B. Priestman Ltd of Hedon Road (regrettably no longer with us) was our biggest and best customer. To that company I feel I owe a debt of gratitude – but then, one good customer does not make a millionaire.

Constantly looking round for other customers and other things to do, led me to try anything and everything that I perceived would make a modest profit, bearing in mind that we were still badly equipped and therefore short on choice. To list the many things I tried without success would only lengthen my story without adding much of interest. One of these ventures, however, was reasonably successful, and that was the production of what is referred to as wrought ironwork, although in fact it is more correctly named decorative metalwork. This refers to the production of metal gates, gateposts, fencing and window grilles. This brought in a modest profit, but it was also important as it was very easy to do and we were well equipped to do it. For some four years or so this kept us ticking over nicely until something more important caught my attention – namely engineering of a more sophisticated sort. This, I am pleased to say, made Turbo Tools a well-known and respected name in over twenty-five countries.

Norman was employed fully on the gates and fencing, doing most of the welding and all of the deliveries. He also undertook to install these products. This he did in his spare time and charged the customers for the privilege, thereby making an extra bob or two for himself.

On one occasion Norman arrived at the home of a customer to install a couple of gateposts. Norman, however, had left his spade at home, but there was nothing very surprising in that. He decided to borrow one from the customer, but unfortunately there was no one at home. Now, there was no way Norman was going to go all that way back home because of such a trifling omission. Looking around, our resourceful, enterprising Norman espied a garden shed and, with caution, tried the door, which to his delight was unlocked. Rummaging through the contents, he found the thing he needed. He completed the task, after which he returned the spade to the shed.

As our friend was tidying up, the customer returned and

66

praised him for a job well done, complimenting him on the manner in which he had made the place tidy and paying him. Before taking his leave Norman apologised for entering the customer's shed and rummaging around without permission. He then thanked him for the loan of the spade, whereupon the customer informed Norman that he did not have a shed and that his spade was in his garage.

While he was telling us this story, Norman said he wondered at the time why the lady next door had taken such an intense interest in his work! In print this little story loses a lot of the humour which accompanied the telling. Thank you, Norman!

Harold was becoming quite useful attending to the wages, preparing invoices and organising transport, as well as other tasks. Unfortunately he was also constantly putting more and more work on to Irene, to such an extent that she very reluctantly decided to retire. She was not at all happy about this as she had enjoyed her involvement. The woman who replaced her came at a price – five times what Irene had been paid for the same job. Although this lady stayed with us for a considerable time, she too eventually left because of the pressures put upon her by Harold. When this happened, our daughter, Margaret, came to work for me. She took complete charge of the office and was admired and respected by all who came into contact with her. Much of my success I owe to her brilliant ability and experience. Prior to taking up her work with me she had been a private secretary to a director at Harlands Printers. She brought with her expertise and professionalism.

For my part, life was getting more and more interesting as things continued to improve. My reputation for designing was spreading and bringing me more business and a better quality of work. I was also being called upon to solve production problems for well-established companies, which thankfully added to my reputation. Among these were names like Blackburn Aircraft, now British Aerospace, J. H. Fenner, J. Reckitt & Sons, and Hull University, and some further afield, such as Keighley Lifts, Baker Perkins, Wilson Gas Meters and many others. Eventually the number of companies in Britain using my equipment were numbered in hundreds. In fact, it is true to say that there is not a single food-producing establishment of any size which does not owe something to Turbo Tools.

As we took on more and more staff we also managed to purchase more and better machines. This inevitably brought the need for more space. Our first move in that direction was to take over the whole of the lower floor of the warehouse. The motor mechanic who shared this with us had decided to move on at just the right time. Before long we occupied the whole of the top part of the building, and soon afterwards we purchased the warehouse along with an old house and yard. So began our purchasing of every small piece of property adjacent to our ramshackle workshop, turning the area into a virtual rabbit warren. This took and lasted a number of years before eventually we had to move, though not before renting and occupying the whole of a derelict church next door.

Some years before we reached this stage I had given a job to another friend of mine. Well, he was a friend when I gave him employment. His name I will not reveal. I had worked with this man earlier, becoming very friendly with him, and I knew him to be a good and skilful worker. From the outset I put him in charge of the maintenance work we were doing for a number of companies. It turned out that he was the first of my employees to do the dirty on me. During the time he was dealing first-hand with these companies he was secretly setting up a business of his own with my customers. In addition he was copying all the tools I had made for the production of the gates and fencing, etc. When he eventually decided to leave, I along with a member of staff called at his workshop and recovered a considerable amount of my equipment. I refused to inform the police, but said a last goodbye to my 'friend'.

Shortly after this our activities at the St George's Road site had changed beyond recognition. No longer were we involved with decorative metalwork or the maintenance work or indeed the subcontract work from J. B. Priestman and the like. We were firmly established as designers and manufacturers of machines for the food and pharmaceutical industries. My introduction to this line of business came about through my involvement with E——.

This man had approached me to help him improve and produce a depositor – a machine which (you've guessed it!) deposited baking materials accurately in the right place at the right time. Now E—— was a baker and he had caught on to the fact that those in his line of business were badly in need of some help. He had a depositor, but it was unreliable. To cut a long story short, after I had completed the work in hand, he asked me to amalgamate with him to form a company for the production of 'bakery machines'. Having had experience as a maintenance engineer at Ernest Ostler's (a local baker's), and having been chief engineer at Clover Dairies, I had some understanding of the food industry and saw the potential immediately. However, I hesitated about taking on another unknown partner who, I might add, came with a reputation, true or false, of unreliability. It did not seem ideal, but this man had a good reputation with bakers and he knew a lot of them.

With all this in mind I made a suggestion that I felt fitted the situation to a tee: I would be responsible for all the design work and Turbo would manufacture all the equipment and sell it to his company strictly at cost, whereupon we would share the profits equally.

For a full year we worked in this manner, although it was not without some controversy. E—— thought he knew better than I did on many occasions. Nevertheless I made sure he failed in his bid to compromise design.

It was during an unexpected visit of mine to the works one Saturday morning (I had taken to having the weekends off) that I was astonished to find E—— showing a competitor around our works. His plan was obvious. I had by this time been made aware of the way he had done things in the past, and this was a clear demonstration of his underhand practices. It was once again goodbye to another 'friendship'.

We never received a penny for the considerable amount of work we did during our first and last year together, but E— was responsible for setting me on the trail that brought us success in the end. It was worth it! The food industry was unbelievably primitive – except, that is, for bread-making. For the rest almost everything was done by hand in a most unhygienic, slow and inaccurate manner. The way to success was handed to me on a plate. Thank you, E—.

Becoming established in the design and manufacture of these specialised machines was not all that easy. It was not possible to drop everything we were doing – we still had a living to make. We were entering an industry where we were quite unknown, in addition to which there were a lot of extra expenses to cope with – for example, the cost of travel, advertising, exhibitions, and brochures for each and every machine we produced – before any sales could be attempted.

Some years earlier I had mortgaged our house for an additional £300. This extra money along with the tools and measuring equipment (worth £400) which was my original investment, combined with my sacrifice of salary for so many years brought my total investment up to a level much higher than that of Harold, though he never seemed to be aware of it. Now we were once again in dire straits for the want of ready cash, and the banks were unsympathetic. This is where Harold proved helpful. He had a sister who to all intents and purposes was a very thrifty lady. He persuaded her to lend us money at an interest rate somewhat higher than she would get elsewhere, though a little less than the banks would have charged. As a matter of fact, out of gratitude to this lady we kept this loan many years after it was really needed. Eventually the bank decided we were not such a bad risk after all, and from then on money was always there when we needed it.

I always begrudged the cost of brochures. It was the high cost of the printing plates (process engraving) which proved to be the main expense. Well, it so happened that we had previously been persuaded to invest a small amount of money in two little ventures that did not materialise. The important thing, however, was that the man involved in these episodes of high finance was a process engraver. His name was Ken. (I have no wish to name him in full.)

It so happened that I knew how printing plates were made, so the high cost gave me the idea that there must be good profits to be made in the printing industry. With this in mind I approached Ken, whom I had recognised as a hard worker, a go-getter and a good craftsman. I hasten to add that he did not mention that at one time he had been declared bankrupt. I persuaded him to forget about the existing ventures and asked him how much money he would require to set up a small process-engraving plant using second-hand machinery, etc. His reply seemed a little on the low side at £400. Nevertheless, Harold and I decided we could just about manage that amount, or perhaps a little more, and I decided we should have a go. It was my decision to proceed with this new venture, as it would be Ken and I who would have to do the work. As it turned out, the initial cost came to over £4,000.

This amount, along with Ken's wages, came as a bit of a drain on our resources. Matters were made even worse when we discovered that we had to buy a house for Ken. You see, the lad lived in York and he had no money. Although Hull Council were accustomed to providing rented accommodation for newcomers who wished to take up work in the city, our application for it was turned down flat. This was perhaps sweet revenge on the part of the council. Perhaps I should deviate a little to explain our chummy relationship with Hull Council.

Our previous request for planning permission was blighted by unwarranted restrictions. The premises in Hawthorn Avenue had been used for light industry for many years, and it was precisely for this purpose that we proposed to use it. Consequently we just had to fight the restrictions. The hassle, the delay and the expense cost us dearly, but we won through in the end. In spite of the unhelpful council we survived.

We gave Ken a one-third share in the new company, also a wage compatible with his previous earnings, and we called the company Trinity Graphic Ltd. There were three of us, you see!

CHAPTER 6

Once all the problems at City Hall had been sorted out, it was all systems go for Ken and me. The new premises in Hawthorn Avenue were not at all suitable for our purposes. Making them suitable was a task which challenged my ingenuity to the full and added to my workload at Turbo, where I already had my hands pretty full. I was dealing at length with customers' special requirements, designing machines (which kept me busy at the drawing board), designing brochures and supervising production. Now, and for the next six months or so, I found myself along with Ken looking for customers. It was somewhat reminiscent of my earlier days with Turbo, although this time I was doing it in style.

It was Margaret's previous employment at Harlands Printers, however, which from the outset tipped the scales in our favour. Through her position as secretary to one of the directors, coupled with the fact that she was well thought of, Ken and I had no difficulty in obtaining as much work as we could handle. For many years Harlands remained our biggest and best customer. I must mention here and now, though, that Ken's knowledge of his subject and his easy manner contributed in no small measure to our success.

With Trinity making all the printing plates, and me doing all the design and layouts for the plates, the cost of the brochures became almost irrelevant. I continued to design the brochures for my machines until my eventual retirement. Although Ken was given the title of managing director, in truth his role was that of technical director. All the managing was done at Turbo, for which we charged a management fee. The wages, the cheques, the purchases, the decisions – with, of course, the consent of the three of us – were all done at Turbo.

Harold and I never took any monies by way of salary, dividends or expenses until some six years or so later, when the company became more profitable. From the beginning Ken was paid a good salary, which increased as things improved. During the early years our commitment to Trinity put an extra drain on our resources, which somewhat hampered developments at Turbo, coming at a time when the demand for more and better equipment seemed to be never-ending. Also, the cost of more advertising, bigger and better exhibitions, increasing travel expenses, etc. all kept our standard of living relatively low. For instance, although we had graduated to having a car each, as opposed to the one we shared for many years, these cars were both second-hand. Even after the first six years we kept our salaries as low as possible, and in consequence our standard of living remained very modest until both ventures were successful.

It was 1970 when we started Trinity in the rented premises in Hawthorne Avenue. As time marched on we bought the property, and years later (1979, to be exact) we were able to build a purposely designed factory further along Hawthorn Avenue, where it remains to this day! With nine momentous years behind us the company went on to achieve a turnover of over £3 million per annum – a tidy sum in 1979 – with excellent profits. Later on a factory in Sarasota, USA was started, along with one in Beijing, China. The old premises, despite their somewhat dilapidated condition, had served us well and were sold.

Trinity Graphic's new factory.

Long before this took place, Turbo Tools had struggled along in the 'rabbit warren' for some eighteen years. During this time we had bought the original two-storey warehouse, three houses, one shop, some old stables and two yards, one of which we made into a workshop, and we had rented two large church halls. Looking back, I find it hard to believe that we were stumbling from one minor crisis to another for so long and in the most difficult surroundings. Those long years, the many changes, all the ups and all the downs, right from the most humble of beginnings in 1957, are now history.

It was 1974 – decision year. It was make-or-break time! Having outgrown the mishmash of workshops, we had to move. The good news was we could afford it – but only just.

All the bits and bobs of land we had purchased were bought by you know who – the council. They bought it for a pittance and, as I recall, did nothing to help us with the high cost of moving. We did it without the slightest help from the council.

Moving lock, stock and barrel presented me with a mountain of extra work, with worry to match. It was essential that we made the move. The state of the offices, which were converted living rooms in what can only be accurately described as a slum, caused me more and more embarrassment as an ever increasing number of customers visited us for consultation. Just as important were the working conditions of the staff. They deserved something a lot better, and it was high time something was done along those lines. Finding a new site, along with the slow negotiations with my 'friends' at the council office, took months, as did the detail planning of the factory itself.

A site situated at the corner of Gillett Street and Hessle Road was, we considered, ideal, and negotiations along with planning went on apace. During this time I had been doing my homework, so to speak! Having visited a few local firms, all of which had recently built factories of their own, I decided that we would do likewise and have a Butler building built. This type of structure was mainly of steel, with walls and roof clad in specially treated sheet aluminium, all of which were prefabricated at the Butler factory – hence the name. These buildings were quick and easy to erect and, in consequence, relatively inexpensive.

As is customary with this sort of activity, but more to keep us on the right side of the building regulations, we employed a professional architect. Did I say professional? This man turned out to be a pain in the proverbial! From the outset he constantly referred to the planned factory as a 'warehouse'. Although this irritated me somewhat, I kept my silence for some considerable time.

My first disagreement with this professional came very early in our discussions. He decided that the Butler building in the form I envisaged would infringe the building regulations and would simply not be allowed. I could not for the life of me understand this. If it was all right for all the other well-established companies in the city, then why not for us? His idea was to construct the whole of one side of the building out of bricks and mortar – a very costly procedure indeed.

Had I given in to this man's ridiculous demands we would have had to drastically modify our plans. To say I was puzzled by his attitude is an understatement. Suffice it to say, I did it my way. It was much, much later in the proceedings, after two more confrontations with the man, that the truth of the situation presented itself. The first of these two confrontations was about the lighting arrangements for the factory (or the warehouse, as he chose to call it). I will spare the reader the boring details, but I halved the cost of the whole extravagant layout. He was not at all pleased. I heard later that he had allowed the supplier of the light fittings to design the layout.

The final episode of this saga was played out when the factory was almost completed. All that remained was the installation of the electrics for the many machines and instruments associated with engineering manufacture. As time went on, I was getting more and more agitated about the delay. The requirements were many and varied, and I did not need to be an expert to realise that such an installation would take a considerable time to complete. The machinery involved ranged from one horsepower to a massive twelve horsepower. Time was marching on.

Turbo Tools' new factory.

Once again I had to talk to my 'adviser'. I informed him that we needed to talk and quickly.

His reply to my request staggered me: "What electrical installation are you talking about? All that has been taken care of," he continued.

I guessed that he must be referring to the lighting arrangements. When I explained about the machinery the tone of his voice said everything. This man thought that we were importers. He could not believe that we were the manufacturers. The constant reference to a warehouse was now explained; it also explained his attitude to the construction of the factory as well as the lighting fiasco.

This man had repeatedly visited our works for long discussions, and our conversations had many times been hindered by the noise from the works, but he had obviously been blind to the reality of the situation. It taught me a lesson with regard to first impressions: it is not what one does in a factory, apparently; it is the appearance of the factory that makes the impression.

It was mid 1975 when we finally moved into our new factory. It was a great day for all of us. The lads to a man, every one of them, had worked very hard to accomplish the move in the shortest time possible. They were and remained a great team. As we went from strength to strength, more and more skilled men joined us, and in spite of their numbers the camaraderie remained – that is with the exception of four of the senior staff, who, I regret to say, plotted in clandestine fashion for at least two years before leaving en masse. As this happened at a much later date, I will explain it in more detail later.

A typical production line for family trifles.

CHAPTER 7

This is a good time, I think, to say a little more about my relationship with the lads. Bearing in mind that I had not been born with a silver spoon in my mouth, I was and still remain sympathetic to those who earn an honest living day in and day out and are contented with their lot. Working in the same environment, doing the same job, does undoubtedly become a little boring at times. Even though they were producing work of a very high standard, it cannot be considered all that exciting.

Because of this, I arranged to have them taken in turn, two at a time, to some of the exhibitions. This gave them a day out and an opportunity to compare their products with those of other manufacturers. This always gave them a bit of a boost. I am not afraid to say it: the superior quality of their efforts was clear for everyone to see. Little enough encouragement, I think, for a deserving workforce! Annually we organised a staff party at a local hotel with food and drink and the price of a taxi there and back. A box of chocolates and a turkey were also part of the festivities. These were good times and I enjoyed them as much as anyone!

This move into the new premises marked the beginning of a new era. Everything seemed to take off from then on. We exhibited in more and more exhibitions all over the world, many in Britain as well as Paris, Munich, Hamburg, Amsterdam, New York, Washington, Chicago, Atlantic City and Tokyo, and cities in Australia, Italy, Spain, Mexico and other countries. All in all we exported to twenty-five countries. In most of these we had agents who had come to us voluntarily. At no time did we seek agents. In fact, there were always agents waiting to handle my machines. With success came more success. No longer were we confined to buying second-hand machinery. Nothing but the latest in computer-controlled high-quality machinery was good enough for yours truly! I still marvel at the transformation in working conditions which we were now beginning to take almost for granted. I had never considered such a situation. When I first set out to have my own little business my thoughts and aspirations were of a far more modest nature. A workforce of half a dozen men in a little workshop was about the limit of my expectations.

With staff numbering close to 100, I was able to leave some of the administration work to others. Margaret by this time had become very efficient at running the office! What a treasure she had turned out to be! No office ever functioned more efficiently than that of Turbo Tools with Margaret at the helm.

All our success, however, did not mean that I was underemployed. It brought with it other problems, and problems meant more work for me. It was I who had to solve all problems, whether technical, legal or other, and always in addition to my design work. For example, there was the time when a French company decided to sue us for something which was way beyond our control.

A Frenchman had acquired two machines from us. These machines were of a very elementary type and quite inexpensive. He then sold them on to a French company, making claims for them which were quite unrealistic. The upshot of this was that the French company tried to recover the cost of the machines, but failed because the Frenchman had gone out of business. The company then tried to get the money out of us, suggesting that the conman was acting as our agent. This was adding insult to injury. We had still not been paid for the machines.

I found the whole business very stressful as there was a lot of money at stake, and things were made much worse because of the language difference, plus the fact that I had to travel to Paris alone to deal with things. I don't know how I did it, but after a lot of travelling, etc., I eventually succeeded in winning the day, though I was somewhat out of pocket.

Now that we had turned the corner (so to speak!) Harold's attitude began to change. Previously he had left everything to me, and gladly, but now as we travelled the world together he resented the attention I was getting from customers. When it came to discussing things of a technical nature he was sadly out of his depth. In spite of this I always included him in any activity where it was possible – so much so that everyone thought he was an engineer who had made significant contributions to our success. I can't help thinking, though, that it was his wife who sowed the seeds of discontent.

Throughout our relationship she had always been unable to disguise her jealousy. Like most women she thought her husband played a greater part in the business than was the case. I considered that to be quite natural and I took no offence. She, however, never openly discussed the situation with me, but regretfully she made Irene the butt of her jealousy. Suffice it to say that the gradual deterioration in our friendship continued for many years before I decided that some drastic action had to be taken.

Eventually she began to complain to me about Harold's trips abroad. Obviously she blamed me for this as I often stayed home while he made overseas visits with members of the sales staff. This put me in a difficult situation. I didn't wish to tell Harold of her complaint and I could not tell her that Harold chose to go on these trips. Frankly, I did not want him to go in the first place as I had had a complaint from one of our agents about his behaviour. (The agent had rung me specifically to ask me to keep him away.) In an attempt to appease his wife and preserve our relationship I encouraged Harold to take his wife with him.

That was a complete failure. After a very expensive trip to the USA, he came back literary empty-handed. A long time later, I was visited by what proved to be a very good customer, and he informed me that he had been unable to make contact with anyone on the stand at the exhibition in New York. It was only by a fluke that this customer contacted me and placed a very good order with us.

Slowly but surely my relationship with Harold worsened. Things finally came to a head in 1979, at a gala dinner in London. An organisation known as Food Europe sent me a letter to the effect that Turbo Tools had been selected for an award. This award was to be presented during a prestigious dinner at the Park Lane Hotel, Park Lane, London. Well, rightly or wrongly I took this to be a tribute to the quality of my machines. After all, I was the designer of the equipment and also the founder of the company. I never thought this was an unreasonable assumption on my part. What is more, I was still doing the lion's share of the work. It certainly did not enter my head that my partner and his wife might have other ideas. As I have said, I had always presented Harold as an equal partner in our company. Never at any time did I even hint to anyone that Harold's contribution was in any way less than my own. Incredibly it seemed as though I had actually convinced Harold that he had contributed as much as I had to our success. It was a good many weeks between receiving the letter regarding the award and the day of the gala dinner. During all this time neither Harold nor his wife so much as hinted that they were not pleased for me to accept the award.

The four of us – Harold, his wife, Irene and I – duly arrived at the selected venue, all set for a wonderful evening together. Everything was proceeding fine until just a few minutes before I was due to go on to the stage.

I was, in fact, just third in line when Harold's wife declared, "Shouldn't you both go up to receive it?"

At this late stage there was no time for a discussion of any sort. I immediately left the table and took up a position where I could see but not be seen, I remained there until, after some slight delay, Harold collected the award *on his own*. Subsequent publicity photographs showed Harold accepting the award, but

editorial office

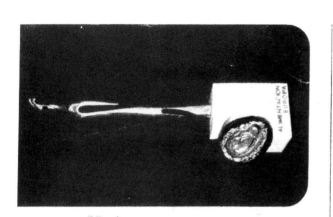

Turbo Tools
Hull, E, Yorkshire (England)

Designers and Manufactures of machinery
For the food and pharmaceutical industries

TURBO TOOLS was started by E fullerton M.Inst.of Patentees & Inventors. Fellow of the Inst. Directors.

Initially this small firm did subcontract work for the larger engineering companies as well as designing and manufacturing one off specialised machines for many industries. It was however in 1968 that Mr Fullerton identified the food Industry as a market crying out for sound ideas and a professional approach to the special problems associated with this industry.

In current production are depositing and filling machines for liquids, creams, fruit and meat products as well as decorating machines for cakes and gateau's: Patented cake cutters and conveyors of advanced design also a range of transfer pumps, multi inline and rotary fillers with cup and foil dispensers and automatic lidding devices.

International
FOOD/EUROPE AWARD

1979

LONDON
15th MARCH. 1979

the name under the photograph was mine. I was sickened by this situation and decided then and there to sell everything, give Harold his full half of the proceeds, and get him and his wife out of my life for ever.

Although I immediately took steps to sell the business, it took a full seven years to find a buyer. Each and every time a prospective buyer was found they backed out when they found that I was due for retirement. This, I think, brought home to Harold the truth of the situation. In spite of everything I felt sorry for him as prospective buyers paid him only polite attention.

The period from 1979 up until the sale of the company and my eventual retirement was punctuated by many changes – some good, some not so good. The worst of the 'not so good' came some time prior to the big sale. A group of conspirators (four in number, three of them in positions of trust, along with a director of a company which had benefited from my patronage) had between them plotted and schemed secretly for two years or more, stealing both materials and drawings and actually manufacturing copies of my machines in our works and in our time. The highlight of their plan was to leave Turbo en masse with the names and addresses of all our customers when they thought the time was ripe, thereby causing us maximum disturbance. Our senior salesman (chief mover, I believe, in this plot) must have thought he was king. The other conspirators – the works manager, the works foreman and a motor mechanic I had befriended – made up this motley crew. During the time this plot was being hatched I was planning to replace the works manager, who was due for retirement, with his co-plotter the works foreman. It was, in fact, just fourteen days before this was about to take place that I was made aware of this cataclysm.

Some time before the works manager was due to retire he had suffered a slight heart attack. At the time it was suggested to me that I retire him there and then. This, however, was not my way of doing things. Instead I undertook some of his duties myself in an endeavour to lighten his load until his eventual leaving. It was about this time that we bought him a new car as a going-away gift. Enough said, for the moment!

In my ignorance I had been grooming the foreman for his new role as manager. As I have explained, it was just two weeks away from the manager's leaving when I received the first indication that I would have to rethink. Having invited the foreman into my office to confirm his new status, I was astonished to be told that he was unable to accept as he was going to start up in business for himself. Even at this stage I had no inkling of what was afoot. After I had recovered from the shock and made it clear to him that I took a dim view about his leaving his announcement so late, I continued with what I thought was a friendly chat about his future plans. Reflecting back on what I had done so many years before, I felt that I was not in a position to take offence. I would add, though, that I left my employer on the very best of terms, and I had no reason to think that the situation here was any different. With this in mind I foolishly told him that I would be able to send him some work which would help him on his way, so to speak, adding that we could remain friends. How he must have been laughing up his sleeve!

Suddenly I had to find another replacement for the works manager, and I had the added task of replacing the foreman and only fourteen days to do it. My first thought was to ask the manager to delay his departure so as to give me a little breathing space. After all, we had always been the best of friends and I had been more than sympathetic after his heart attack. His refusal both hurt and puzzled me, though it didn't puzzle me for long. There was worse to come.

I cannot remember exactly when it was that the senior salesman came along and had the audacity to offer me one month's notice of termination of his contract. As I recall, I sacked him on the spot, along with the semi-skilled motor mechanic. I now had to do a lot of salvage work!

Having rid myself of this devious bunch of individuals, I

remained unaware of the vast scale of the betrayal. They themselves, however, provided the proof. Within two months of leaving our employ they were offering a machine for sale. It was obvious therefore that this machine had been in the making for at least two years. Such a machine would take at least that amount of time to plan and produce even if they had had the plant and the staff, which they did not have in any measure. They were, in fact, advertising their treachery for all to see. Apart from the evidence which I eventually accumulated, the case against them was already substantial and proven.

The reader may well speculate as to why, with such a strong case against them, Subversive Engineering (as I choose to call them) were not called to account for their blatant, gross dishonesty. To attempt to answer this in detail would serve no useful purpose and would perhaps be boring. It is well known that legal action of this sort is both expensive and takes a long time, the long time being the main thing that let them off the hook.

When legal action against them was coming to an end, the company had been sold, Harold had been paid in full (an amount equal to the sum I had received) and he was now no longer involved. I had been retained on a two-year contract, with the proviso that the contract would be renewed if I so chose. The position of chairman on a part-time basis at a salary of £25,000 per annum pleased me very much. In completion of the deal, Harold and I received half the sale price in cash and half in shares of the company making the purchase.

Everything was going well. I was getting along very nicely with United Spring & Steel, the new owners of Turbo, and we were all looking forward to the pending action with regard to Subversive Engineering. It was then that the unexpected happened: United Spring & Steel was taken over by a much larger company (the word 'speculator' comes to mind). From that very moment things started to go hopelessly wrong. This self-opinionated whizz-kid of an accountant took over and made many changes, none of which could be considered as for the better. For some reason, this man took an instant dislike to me and he never spoke to me except under duress. I have realised since that this man did not know I was the designer of all the equipment. You see, in later years I did not put my name at the bottom of the drawings as the designer. I did not think it necessary, although I allowed the man who did the drawings to do so. Never once did he ever talk to me about the company. It was obvious from the outset that when my contract came to an end I would be out on my ear, and I was. There was, in fact, no limit to this man's talents. In no time at all the shares in this all-powerful company dropped from £1.60 per share to eighty pence per share. Unfortunately, I had over 600,000 of them. My losses at that time were in the region of £912,000, and there was worse to come.

The company had to be sold off to avoid further losses and my shares, which once stood at over £960,000 were eventually reduced to around £12,000. Added to this was my loss of salary plus the loss of £15,000 per annum dividends on my shares before their demise, making an additional loss of £40,000 per annum. Turbo had already been sold at a loss.

I'm racing on a bit here, but before I return to the Subversive Engineering saga, the reader will see that I had no reason to trust or be at all fond of this accountant, who from the outset seemed to me to be very much out of his depth. If my memory serves me correctly, this took place around 1989 – not a very good year for me. It was, however, just prior to the financial collapse that Mr Clever Clogs, with his almost paranoid dislike for me, made it clear that he thought my action against Subversive Engineering was a waste of time and money. By now, though, it looked as though he was not too sure of himself. Was he losing confidence? It would seem so, as he decided, along with his sidekick the managing director, to accompany me on a prearranged visit to our barrister in London.

Mr Clever Clogs was taken aback by this encounter, with the result that he not only agreed to proceed with the action, but he was positively in favour of it. For the first time he began to realise the benefit this would be to the company. He did not allow this to bring him down from his high horse, though – no, sir. On the return train journey he made it quite clear that I was not good enough; nor was I welcome to share his company – he left me to make the rail journey back alone.

It was this final rebuff that really upset me – so much so that I decided to withdraw my support. In view of the long, hard, expensive fight it was not an easy decision to make, but I could not see myself receiving a fair deal from this arrogant, insensitive man and I was determined therefore that he would not benefit. I think Mr Clever Clogs was peeved!

That is how and why Subversive Engineering was let off the hook. It does not mean, however, that I can easily forgive or forget. Their action cost me dearly. Hitherto I had no competition, and because of that I would have received much more for the company when it was sold. Their very existence, along with their unscrupulously exaggerated claims regarding their positions at Turbo – claims made to our customers whenever it suited their aims – regrettably had an effect on our business.

Another type of trifle production line.

CHAPTER 8

Although I have worked hard all my life (indeed very little has come easily), I felt at all times that I have on the whole been fortunate. However, as we all know the summer sun must eventually make way for a little rain. Sad to say, the rain started for me a couple of years prior to the devastation wrought by the infamous Mr Clever Clogs.

Some considerable time before the event which I am about to describe we had set up a pension scheme for the staff of both our companies. It was Harold's responsibility to administer this scheme, but, as was Harold's way, he quickly passed the job over to a member of staff who was fully occupied with more technical tasks. When therefore Harold informed me that he had been approached by what seemed to be a professional organisation to take over the running of the scheme I readily agreed.

Once again this could be a long story. Suffice it to say that this *professional* organisation turned out to be a group of embezzlers, four of whom were sent to jail, but not before causing me a lot of extra work (which I could have well done without). More importantly, some of the staff lost pension rights and I lost a large part of my own pension. At the time the police considered that Harold was involved in the conspiracy, but as I had no evidence of this I persuaded them that he was not. I never mentioned this episode to Harold. This event was the first of my series of misfortunes.

It was during the crisis of Mr Clever Clogs that I lost my right eye. Well, I did not lose it exactly – I always knew where it was – but I did become blind in that eye. It started with what seemed to be a slight shadow in the eye. Subsequent tests proved it to be a detached retina.

At first I was not too concerned. I had heard of many such cases which had not proved to be all that serious. Why mine went so wrong I don't know, but I lost the sight completely after two lengthy operations. That was a misfortune in itself, but if it had happened just nine months sooner, when a long-standing insurance policy was in place, I would have at least been compensated to the tune of £20,000. These were misfortunes number three and four. Having been literally kicked out of Turbo, I now decided to retire completely.

Gradually I am becoming accustomed to being a one-eyed Cyclops. For instance, at the dinner table I am much more careful when pouring out the wine. I don't always miss the glass as I did at the beginning. Looking on the bright side (that's my left side!) there are some compensations. For instance I need only clean one lens when giving my spectacles a spring clean, and I can sleep with one eye open if I try hard enough!

Seeking to become a man of leisure, I decided to offer Harold my shares in Trinity Graphic Ltd. This was a golden opportunity for Harold: he would be in sole control of the company. The company would be his.

I should mention that throughout our association Harold and Ken (the other director of Trinity) had always been the very closest of friends, much to my exclusion. Sharing similar tastes and aspirations, they had through the years involved themselves in a number of schemes designed specifically for their own benefit, all at the expense of the company. For instance, they bought a large yacht on the pretext that it was to entertain customers. Although I agreed to the purchase, solely to keep them happy, it was not my cup of tea, and at the time I did not expect the escalating expense of the refit. However, that's another story. All in all I got nothing out of that situation, but I did not mind all that much. The one scam that did hurt me somewhat was one in which between them they set up a company along with an artist fellow who was the son of a well-known – indeed, famous – artist.

The object of this company was to produce high-quality prints of this man's paintings. It was envisaged that the original would then become inflated in value by extensive marketing of the prints. Needless to say, Harold bought the original, and as part of the deal agreed to give this artist fellow a full fifty per cent of the company, leaving the remainder to be shared between the two of them. All of this was done in the utmost secrecy, despite the fact that the technical work and all the printing was being done at Trinity, with me as the unsuspecting contributor. It was only when it became obvious that things were not going to plan that I was unceremoniously included in the scheme as though I had been part of it from the outset. The reader may think I was a fool to let things ride, but I did, for I had already decided to part company with Harold and I was too busy to fight anyway.

I was therefore very surprised when, after offering Harold my shares in Trinity, Ken came round to see me in haste. He was in a right old state. The long and the short of it was that he was devastated by the very thought that Harold might take control of the company, and he pleaded with me at great length to change my mind. When it came to putting self-interest first I was never a good businessman, and this is when I made the second big mistake of my life (my first mistake being the sale of Turbo). I agreed that Trinity Graphic should buy Harold's shares.

This effectively meant that Ken and I became equal shareholders in that company. As I look back I find it hard to believe that I could have been so stupid. I sold Turbo mainly for Harold's benefit, and here I was again making a similar mistake for the sake of Ken. Together these two mistakes eventually changed the whole of my life, regrettably not for the better.

Blissfully unaware of the error of my ways, I had committed myself to a continued involvement with the company and Ken. It was certainly not the way I had planned things originally. To make the best of a bad job, I employed a qualified full-time accountant to alleviate some of the tedium and allow me more time to myself. After all, I was supposed to be in retirement. For the first couple of years or so things went reasonably well. Then things started to happen. Without my knowledge or consent, Ken had committed us to two ventures which I believe were the commencement of our slide down the slippery slope of adversity. In truth, I must add that there were other factors which contributed to the slide; without them we might have side-stepped the impending disaster. These other factors will be revealed as my sad story unfolds.

CHAPTER 9

The ventures to which I referred were the setting up of two more companies – one in Sarasota, USA and the other in Beijing, China. The Beijing company was in conjunction with the Chinese Government, and was quite a good move. Indeed, had it not been for some of the other factors appertaining at the time, it would have been very successful. Unfortunately, the factory in Sarasota became a never-ending drain on our finances. Ken had installed his son over there to run the company, and, having spent so much money, it was difficult to know if or when to withdraw support. It was a difficult situation by any standard, but we could have survived. The bank was willing to lend us the money provided we both gave our personal guarantees, which we did. In spite of the fact that the whole process-engraving industry was going through a technical revolution, and a costly one at that, I was convinced that all would be well given a little time.

I was completely unaware at this stage that Ken had been up to more of his clandestine tricks, and I was about to find out the hard way. Although profits had taken a downturn owing to all the extra investment we were making, I was sure we were coming out of it gradually. My first intimation of impending disaster was when I discovered that Ken had raised his salary to a level higher than that of the prime minister. Further investigation revealed that he had secretly been running another business, with the result that he was neglecting the responsibilities for which he was so highly paid. Other ramifications of his misconduct had all contributed to a very dangerous situation, and the time of reckoning had arrived.

I now found that the bank held me responsible not only for my share of the borrowings but also for Ken's share. Added to this was the fact that the increase in his salary was for no other reason but to help pay off a debt which was threatening him with bankruptcy. I was devastated. I had always treated borrowing with the utmost caution, but I now felt the closeness of the cold wind of bankruptcy for the very first time. Drastic action was called for and quickly. The bank was still willing to lend us money on my guarantee, but I refused this point-blank and immediately put the company up for sale.

The long drawn-out procedure which ensued was very time-consuming and gave me real cause for worry. The company at that time was estimated to be worth close to £3 million, but by the time the accountants had finished with it I felt lucky that we had cleared all the debts. I received not a penny. The Hull company was sold for just a fraction of its true value, as indeed was the one in the USA. That one I sold to Ken's son, who I expect and hope is benefiting from it to this day. As far as I know the China project was simply abandoned in favour of the Chinese, and rightly so. What I do know is that no profit from that enterprise ever appeared in the books of Trinity Graphic.

Obviously the collapse of my remaining asset had a profound effect on our standard of living. We could no longer afford the upkeep of the large and beautiful house in Kirk Ella, and my Rolls-Royce Silver Spirit had to be sold. Mind you, this was partly because of its size, and after losing my right eye I was finding it a little difficult to manage. It also looked a bit ostentatious outside the smaller home to which we reluctantly had to move.

In spite of this I remain, as always, able to count my blessings. Perhaps I was never meant to be really wealthy. I have my health and strength and enough income to remain comfortable – not everyone is so blessed. It would, however, have been nice if I had saved a little more, allowing me to give a little more help to others. Frankly, the loss of the money is not of any great concern to me. I have to confess, however, that a little more recognition of my work, especially in the food industry, would not have gone amiss.

With the string of misfortunes behind me – the loss of part of my pension, the loss of my eye, the loss of my job at Turbo coupled with the crash of my shares in that company and (what I thought was the final catastrophe) the loss of Trinity Graphic – Irene and I settled down to what we thought would be a modest but nice retirement. We soon became accustomed to our new situation, and we were indeed very happy with our new home. This we thought was to be our Serendipity, our Last Repose. It was September 1991.

Irene, me, Charles, Margaret and little Richard.

Fate, however, had decided otherwise. After a fleeting seven years of happiness, on the evening of 6 November 1998, a date indelibly etched on my memory, disaster struck – a disaster surpassing all others. My dear sweet Irene suffered a severe stroke which left her paralysed down her right-hand side and, worst of all, unable to speak. After a dreadful long spell in hospital the doctors decided there was no indication that her condition would ever improve; she would be badly disabled for the rest of her life. This was very hard to bear. I realised immediately that due to my wartime back injury I could not cope on my own. Inevitably she would have to reside for the rest of her days in a care home.

The following days turned to weeks as my daughter Margaret and I, along with a nursing friend of Margaret's, toured the area looking for suitable accommodation. All during this time my dear Irene was incarcerated in the local hospital. I use the word 'incarcerated' because of my observations during my long daily visits to that uninviting place. The first few weeks of Irene's stay in hospital were of the highest standard and I am ever thankful for the care and attention she received at the hands of the very busy doctors and staff at that time. Regrettably as the weeks went by I became aware of what I perceived to be a change in the attitude of some doctors and certainly the senior staff. The ward Irene was in was populated in the main by older people, many of whom were in a similar position to Irene, and, quite frankly, the staff were doing their best to get these patients out of their beds and into nursing homes or care homes.

I was spending the biggest part of every day with Irene, and in consequence had ample time to observe the manner in which they were trying to achieve this. For instance, there were a number of male mental patients all wandering around the ladies' ward, much to the distress of the ladies, though there was ample room in the men's ward for these very poorly individuals. There were other things that I found hard to stomach. One doctor instructed a member of the senior staff to interfere between me and the matron of a nursing home in which we were trying to place Irene. The very cheek of the man! I had the unpleasant task of sorting him out, along with his lackey. I also took the opportunity to mention my other observations, which I am pleased to say resulted in a change for the better with regard to the other patients – possibly, though, only temporary.

Many of the homes we visited did not seem right for Irene,

but eventually we settled on one in the centre of Cottingham. It was a care home – not a nursing home, which the doctor had gone out of his way to recommend. I think someone up there had been guiding us, for we could not have made a better choice. The name of this place was The Maples Care Home, and The Maples very soon became almost as much a home to me as it did to Irene. To Andrea Steele (the proprietor), Diana Kirk (the manageress) and their dedicated staff I am, and will always remain, eternally grateful.

Due to the loss of sight in one eye I was finding it difficult driving all the way from Kirk Ella to Cottingham four times every day, especially at night. I was scared stiff that even a slight accident could interfere with my visits. Such a thing would have devastated Irene, and I could not risk it. It was this that made me decide to sell the bungalow in Kirk Ella as soon as we had settled Irene in The Maples. This in itself was a hard decision for me. Irene had loved this last place, which, although smaller than our previous home, was in fact quite roomy. I now realised that my life had changed completely. No longer would I need or favour a house so large. I was already on my own, and that was how it was going to stay. In addition, these changes meant I would be leaving behind all my friends. I wasn't looking forward to the upheaval at all. But it had to be – I would have to move to Cottingham.

These were dreadful times. I dared not contemplate the future. Taking one day at a time was about all I could manage. Each day at around ten in the morning I would visit Irene, and I would always have lunch with her – a lunch that was never charged for, courtesy of those lovely people at The Maples. After lunch I would go home to return again in the early evening and stay until around nine o'clock. Each day when it was not raining I would take Irene out in her wheelchair until it was time for lunch, and I am pleased to say that I was able to visit her every single day for just over two years until her sudden and unexpected passing.

The daily excursions with Irene in her wheelchair caused

me to become very familiar with the geography of Cottingham, a place I have come to love and one in which I have found good neighbours. They have been an enormous help. A big thank you therefore to the Shearmans, the Barretts, the Delaneys, the Liggins, the Spivys, the Garmstons, the Macmanuses and the Wilsons.

Regrettably, moving to Cottingham was more of an upheaval than I could ever have imagined. Once more fate took a hand – and it was not a helping hand. Having found suitable accommodation, I obtained a bridging loan from the bank to cover me for the short time it would take me to sell the property in Kirk Ella. I was confident that it would be for no more than six weeks at the most, and, true to my expectations, the first people to view the house decided to buy. It should have been only a few weeks before the deal was done and I would be free to settle down to my new situation. It was then that the bombshell fell!

The reader may or may not know of a condition known as sulphate attack, which undermines building foundations. This is about the very worst thing that can happen to a house. If it is left unchecked, the house will literally fall apart, and the cost of putting the problem right can be in the region of £40,000–£50,000. What is more, it is normally not covered by insurance and can take (as it eventually did in our case) up to ten months to remedy.

In spite of the fact that I had a survey done before purchasing the house, specifically to ensure that it was clear of any such potentially devastating defects (perhaps I should mention here that many of my neighbours' properties had already suffered from this malaise), I was now told that the foundations had the dreaded defect and that the place was unsaleable in its present state.

This overwhelming news could not have come at a worse time. So many other things were claiming my attention that I just do not know how I managed to cope. Fortunately the buyer agreed to complete the purchase, but not until all the building work had been completed, the whole house redecorated, and the buyer given a certificate of completion. During the whole of this time – ten months, as I recall – I was paying the bridging-loan interest, which in the end left me some £12,000 out of pocket.

These continued demands on my dwindling capital did nothing for my peace of mind. Where would it all end? I was still out on a limb and very worried. Would the insurance company pick up the bill for the very expensive work now in progress, or would they not? What a great relief it was when the good news eventually came! As it turned out, the problem had been caused in the first place by a faulty drain, and the company accepted responsibility. The long weeks of waiting and worrying had come to an end. Would this also be the end of my long run of misfortune?

While all this was going on I was sorting out my new bungalow. It was very much smaller than the previous one, which meant that I had to dispose of many items of furniture. Disposing of the baby grand piano was without doubt the one thing that hurt me the most. Irene was a very accomplished pianist, and the piano, one could say, was a part of her – it was entirely hers. It broke my heart when I had to part with it. Furthermore I could not tell her the truth; nor did I enjoy telling her the white lie that I had temporarily put it in storage. That, in fact, was just a small lie compared with the one I told her regarding my change of abode. I was fearful that she would realise her condition was permanent, so I told her I was renting a smaller house in Cottingham. I further lied that until things improved I had rented out the house she loved. Three big lies in a row – is it always a sin to tell a lie?

My move into Cottingham took place in March 2000, a year which, without exception, was the most difficult in the whole of my life. As the year slowly came to its end, all the difficulties with regard to moving house were behind me and the saga of the house that was about to fall down was over. All these problems were now behind me and I could concentrate on looking after my dear wife. Life was not too easy, but I saw people with greater problems than mine and I was grateful.

Early one morning in the year 2001 (20 January, to be exact), just thirteen months since the termination of my recent problems, I was awakened by the sound of the doorbell. Standing at my door was my daughter, Margaret, and her husband, Charles. Seeing them both together and so early in the morning told me immediately that something dreadful was about to unfold. It was Margaret who had the thankless task of informing me of my dear wife's sudden passing. Alone in a strange bed, and in her sleep, she had quietly returned to heaven. When I had tucked her up in bed for the night, as I did every night, little did I know that when I said goodnight it was also goodbye. For some time in the following years depression was to be my constant companion.

There is little else to say now, except that I was absolutely penniless when I started my sometimes trying, but most times exciting, journey. I have some regrets, but only a few. The good times greatly outnumber the not so good. We, Irene and I, cruised first class on the *QE2* some twenty-one times; also on the *Canberra* and the *Vistafjord*; we flew by Concorde to the USA some seven times. On one special occasion we flew to New York, had lunch on the *QE2* (which was in New York Harbour at the time), and flew back home on Concorde on the very same day!

We also dined with Her Majesty The Queen Mother, Princess Margaret, Princess Anne, Prince Edward, Prince and Princess Michael of Kent, Lord Snowdon, and Lord and Lady Tavistock, all on different occasions. We have enjoyed the company of many television and film personalities, including Anna Neagle, Vera Lynn, Arthur Tracy, Ruby Keeler, Jimmy Tarbuck, Bruce Forsyth, Bob Hope, Robert Powell, Margaretta Scott, Hughie Green, Tom O'Connor, Bob Monkhouse, Iris Williams, Jimmy Savile, Frankie Howerd, Joe Loss and Douglas Bader (the legless pilot). I have seen sunrises on the other side of the world, along with unforgettable sunsets. I have been very sad at times, but more often tremendously happy, and I had a wonderful marriage.

Captain's cocktail party on the QE2,
me, Margaret, Irene and Charles, 1979.

As I write this, the end of my story, in the year 2003, I am halfway into my eighty-third year. It is ironical, (is it not?) that this very day I read in the *Hull Daily Mail,* that work is to start on the demolition of the Regal Cinema – the very place where my working life started! It is a pity, I think – not only because of my memories of the place, but because it is a fine building, not at all like the new and drooled-over monstrosity housing The Deep. A real blot on the landscape if ever there was one!

For those who may not be familiar with the recent developments in Hull, The Deep is an aquarium of sorts. Although quite a popular and interesting attraction, it is housed in what to me looks more like a huge pile of scrap metal than a building. I can't help wondering just how long such a ghastly structure can survive.

On a recent visit to my old company, my good friends there told me there are now many companies making my equipment (most of them had a close business relationship with me in the past). It is said that throughout the world these machines are almost always referred to as Turbo machines. Perhaps I have made a mark after all.

Although I have lost a lot of money, I am better off than I was at the beginning. I have enough of my pension left to live in reasonable comfort, and I have been able to help my small family. For that and many other things I am most grateful. If I were ever asked to say anything to the young just starting out on their journey, it would be "One does not have to win all the battles in life to remain happy."

Life before the troubles, 1989.

One of our many exhibition stands.

A typical production line for the production of family trifles.

MY HISTORY IN BRIEF

Left school at the age of fourteen.

Eventually trained as an engineering craftsman, became proficient at fitting, turning, all types of machining, welding, etc., and technical drawing.

Spent two years as shift manager in the die-casting department of Armstrong Patents (shock absorbers).

Spent three years as works manager for Dura Products (domestic fittings).

Spent three years as chief engineer at a local bakery.

Spent four and a half years as chief engineer at Clover Dairies, Hull, Grimsby and Scunthorpe.

Founded an engineering company for the design and manufacture of specialised machinery. Customers included Rolls-Royce, Hepworth & Grandage, J. H. Fenner, Priestman Brothers, Rapistan, Reckitt & Coleman, Portasilo, British Aerospace (formerly Blackburn Aircraft) and many others. My company exported to over twenty countries worldwide, including the USA and Japan. In addition to the design and manufacture of jigs and tools for British Aerospace, I spent much time at the factory supervising the making-out of job sheets and methods of manufacture on a day-to-day basis, spread over eighteen months.

Designed and manufactured the world's first precision positioner, for use with turret presses, and nibbling machines. This was the machine that made CNC high-speed punching, etc. possible. It has been recognised as the greatest breakthrough in the history of sheet-metal working.

Founded a successful process-engraving company with branches in Hull, Sarasota (USA) and Beijing (in partnership with the Chinese Government).

ACHIEVEMENTS

Created getting on for 100 manufacturing jobs in Hull.

Revolutionised the hygiene standard and production costs of convenience foods.

Had exhibitions in New York, Washington, Atlantic City and Sarasota (all USA), three cities in Germany, two in Holland, one in France, one in Italy and one in Japan. I was visited in Hull by representatives from all of these countries, seeking agencies to sell my machines.

Filed over thirty patent applications to date.

Broadcast on BBC radio on two occasions.

Appeared on BBC's *Tomorrow's World* and on Yorkshire Television.

Lectured at the Thomas Danby College, Leeds, and at the London Polytechnic.

Became a member of the Institute of Patentees and Inventors.

Was for three years president of the Hull Association of Engineers.

Became a fellow of the Institute of Directors.

Granted life membership of the RAF association.

Included in *Debrett's Distinguished People of Today* (1990), the *Dictionary of International Biography* and the *International Who's Who of Professionals*.

Became a member of the National Geographic Society.

SOME OF MY INVENTIONS

Safety stop for ladders, February 1953 – Pat. 4425/53.

Dead man's brake for prams, lawnmowers and railway trolleys, 1956 – Pat. 12862/56.

Electric plug-in timer, 1958 (never patented because of bad advice from the patent agent, Cottrell).

False fingernails, 1968.

Pantograph (precision positioner), August 1968 – Pat. 39687/68 and (1969) Pat. 39507/67.

Vibrazor cake cutter, 1970.

Quick-release conveyor belts, 1970.

Nailing machine for printing plates, March 1970 – Pat. 13667/70.

Disposable plastic gloves, July 1970 – Pat. 36613/70.

Inline filling machine, March 1972 – Pat. 9505/72.

Rigid plastic insert for easy filling of flimsy plastic bin bags,

August 1972 – Pat. 9216825.

Agitator for food products, 1973.

Automatic machine for depositing continuous layers of food products, 1977 – Pat. 222191/77.

Safety drive arrangement for rotary indexing table, December 1980 – Pat. GB 2 065 830 A.

Pie-filling depositor, January 1981.

Filler for foaming liquids, January 1982.

Continuous filler for ice cream, 1982 – Pat. GB 2 131 006 A.

Container-filling apparatus, April 1983 – Pat. 2133 791 A.

Full cover nozzles (food stuffs), 1986.

Suck-back nozzle for viscous fluids (now used in honey bottles), 1986.

Full spread nozzles (jam, cream and the like), 1986.

Lidding machine, August 1988 – Pat. 8819745.4.

Device for filling wide-necked containers, August 1988 – Pat. 8820202.3.

Rapid cut-off nozzles, August 1988 – Pat. 8819746.2.

Electrical test plug, January 1990 – Pat. 9002166.8.